C000246765

ASIA SMALL AND MEDIUM-SIZED ENTERPRISE MONITOR 2021

VOLUME IV—PILOT SME DEVELOPMENT INDEX:
APPLYING PROBABILISTIC PRINCIPAL
COMPONENT ANALYSIS

APRIL 2022

ASIAN DEVELOPMENT BANK

Contents

Tables and Figures

Foreword

I n 2020, the Asian Development Bank (ADB) began designing a benchmark index to measure the level of micro, small, and medium-sized enterprise (MSME) development by using a multivariate analytical approach based on real country data—called the Small and Medium-Sized Enterprise Development Index (SME-DI). The concept is based on the question: why do constraints remain on MSME development in most countries despite government attempts over the past decades to promote MSME development?

The limited availability of MSME data makes it difficult for governments to design an appropriate MSME policy. ADB's Asia Small and Medium-Sized Enterprise Monitor (ASM) was created in part to deal with these data limitations and help governments promote evidence-based policymaking on MSME development and access to finance. Designing an SME-DI at the regional and national levels is part of the ASM project. It is expected to allow for a more solid means of evaluating MSME development by using real data and advanced econometrics.

The SME-DI is an ambitious and challenging initiative. This report—Volume IV of the ASM 2021—presents a new pilot of the SME-DI that fills in missing data on MSMEs by using a probabilistic principal component analysis model. Pilot testing was used to generate a regional SME-DI for 15 ASM participating countries from Southeast Asia and South Asia, based on the 2021 ASM database. A country-level SME-DI was constructed for Viet Nam using firm-level data obtained from the country's business registration data.

We will continue to strengthen our ASM database by gathering a wider range of aggregate- and firm-level data about MSMEs from our developing member countries. This will enable us to continue to apply the model to different countries at various levels to increase the validity of the SME-DI and make it a more valuable tool to support policymakers.

Albert Park
Chief Economist and Director General
Economic Research and Regional Cooperation Department
Asian Development Bank

Acknowledgments

The Asia Small and Medium-Sized Enterprise Monitor (ASM) 2021 Volume IV was prepared by Shigehiro Shinozaki, senior economist, Economic Research and Regional Cooperation Department (ERCD) of the Asian Development Bank (ADB) and Daisuke Miyakawa, chief economist, UTokyo Economic Consulting Inc. (UTEcon). The research was assisted by Keiichi Goshima, Kazusato Oko, and Hiroki Matsumoto, from the UTEcon. Administrative support was provided by Richard Supangan and Maria Frederika Bautista.

The country Small and Medium-Sized Enterprise Index (SME-DI) model was run using micro, small, and medium-sized enterprise (MSME) data extracted from business registration data received from Viet Nam's Agency for Business Registration. We very much appreciate its support for this SME-DI project.

In 2021, we also concluded the agreement with Credit Bureau Cambodia (CBC) led by Sothearoath Oeur, chief executive officer of CBC, to further develop the country's SME-DI by expanding use of granular MSME data. However, due to the coronavirus disease (COVID-19) pandemic, we faced a critical issue on virtual data sharing between ADB and CBC teams. Thus, this report does not include the updated SME-DI for Cambodia. We hope to continue our collaboration with CBC for this initiative.

Abbreviations

ABR	—	Agency for Business Registration (Viet Nam)
ADB	—	Asian Development Bank
ASEAN	—	Association of Southeast Asian Nations
ASM	—	Asia Small and Medium-Sized Enterprise Monitor
CBC	—	Credit Bureau Cambodia
COVID-19	—	coronavirus disease
EM	—	expectation-maximization
GFC	—	2008–2009 global financial crisis
GDP	—	gross domestic product
MSME	—	micro, small, and medium-sized enterprise
NPL	—	nonperforming loan
OECD	—	Organisation for Economic Co-operation and Development
PC	—	principal component
PCA	—	principal component analysis
SME-DI	—	Small and Medium-Sized Enterprise Development Index

Executive Summary

Governments across developing Asia continue to look for a way to summarize the business activities of micro, small, and medium-sized enterprises (MSMEs). A proper summary would be extremely useful when crafting policies to encourage MSME market access, entrepreneurship, use of technology, commercialization, and access to financing. To help respond to this need, this report constructs a Small and Medium-Sized Enterprise Development Index (SME-DI) that reflects lessons learned from the preliminary SME-DI exercise ADB conducted in 2020 (ADB 2020).

Despite broad agreement on the need for an SME-DI, two major issues need to be resolved. First, there is the general lack of data. The second is how best to use existing data, which is why we remain at an early stage in developing an effective index. As datasets strengthen and deepen, we will be better able to develop a more useful and feasible SME-DI. The actual data remain sparse, based on what we need to properly estimate and interpret the SME-DI. Thus, a new model that helps deal with missing data can enhance the accuracy of the SME-DI.

To do this, after reviewing the 2020 SME-DI exercise, this study proposes a principal component analysis (PCA) variant that can run given current data limitations. After describing the data, we estimate the pilot SME-DI using a probabilistic PCA method and a standard PCA method, and interpret the results.

In our first attempt, we developed a regional SME-DI using country-level panel data from our Asia SME Monitor 2021 database. The dataset covers 15 countries—10 from Southeast Asia (Brunei Darussalam, Cambodia, Indonesia, the Lao People's Democratic Republic [Lao PDR], Malaysia, Myanmar, the Philippines, Singapore, Thailand, and Viet Nam) and five from South Asia (Bangladesh, India, Nepal, Pakistan, and Sri Lanka). The study found that from 2009 to 2020, the Asian region covering these 15 countries suffered from the 2008–2009 global financial crisis (GFC) that led to an increase in nonperforming loans, and then experienced recoveries in the capital markets and the status of corporate finance. In effect, the GFC slowed MSME development until 2014 as nonperforming MSME loans increased and the number of MSMEs decreased. However, a recovery in capital markets and MSME financing began between 2013 and 2015, with new finance available for MSME development afterward.

Breaking down the results by subregion, in Southeast Asia, from the GFC to 2014, Malaysia and the Philippines contributed to region's increased nonperforming MSME loans. Decreased MSME exports (by value) in Malaysia and Thailand also hurt MSME development in the region. From 2013 to 2015, a recovery in capital markets, especially in markets catering to growth-related firms—including MSMEs (mai in Thailand and Catalist in Singapore)—contributed to a recovery of the region's MSMEs. After 2016, MSME development in the region was supported by increasing number of MSMEs in Indonesia and Viet Nam; more nonbank loans in Viet Nam, Cambodia, and the Philippines; and increased MSME value-added in terms of gross domestic product (GDP) in Indonesia and Thailand.

In South Asia, nonperforming MSME loans in Pakistan and lower MSME export values in India slowed the region's MSME development in the aftermath of the GFC. From 2012 to 2015, however, a recovery of capital markets in

Pakistan and Sri Lanka, decreased nonbank finance nonperforming loans in Bangladesh and Sri Lanka, increased MSME employment in India, and rising contributions to GDP from small manufacturing firms in Pakistan helped South Asia's MSME sector recover. After 2016, increased MSME bank loans in India and Bangladesh, nonbank loans in Pakistan and Sri Lanka, and a rise in the number of MSMEs in Nepal supported South Asia's MSME development.

The regional SME-DI suggests that equity finance was likely critical in bringing about the recovery of the MSME sector from the crisis. Once recovered, it was bank credit and nonbank finance that likely supported further MSME development. This suggests that finance remains critical to MSME development. In particular, the availability of growth capital best facilitated their recovery and growth. This is consistent with the key findings from the Asia SME Monitor 2021 Volume 1 that stressed the need for more growth capital for MSMEs during a post-pandemic recovery.

In our second attempt, we also developed a country-level SME-DI using firm-level panel data from Viet Nam's Agency for Business Registration. We found that MSMEs in Viet Nam over the 3 years from 2017 to 2019 had continuous sales growth in manufacturing, trade, and transport, and higher employment in trade and agri-food services. Profitability, especially in construction, improved briefly, followed by a slight drop. MSME development was backed by new infrastructure needs and a national procurement law preferential to domestic bidding by small firms, allowing MSMEs in construction to participate in small infrastructure projects.

While this regional and country-specific exercise helped construct a SME-DI, there remain some important issues. First, more data, especially granular firm-level data, need to be used under the proposed framework to estimate factors that represent MSME activities. Second, we must continue test runs for various countries at various levels, such as at the aggregate- and firm-levels. Third, after confirming the validity of the SME-DI, it should be used to predict some important aspects such as MSME contributions to GDP. Regardless of whether the SME-DI is used for current results or as a forecast, a concisely summarized SME-DI is a useful analytical tool to help governments better design evidence-based MSME policies.

Introduction

In 2020, the Asian Development Bank (ADB) began to design a benchmark index to numerically measure the level of micro, small, and medium-sized enterprise (MSME) development. The Small and Medium-Sized Enterprise Development Index (SME-DI) used a multivariate analytical approach based on real country data. The idea was to determine why constraints on MSME development remain in most countries across the region, despite government policies over the past decades to promote MSME development. One critical factor was the lack of data and information on MSMEs, making it difficult to design workable MSME policies. In fact, limited data availability and their comparability make a real data evaluation of MSME development extremely difficult both nationally and regionally. To more accurately identify the structural problems MSMEs face, this study takes the SME-DI further.

With continuous pilot testing, the study moved to its second phase in 2021 to develop an analytical model in cooperation with the UTokyo Economic Consulting Inc. The ADB 2020 Asia Small and Medium-Sized Enterprise Monitor (ASM) highlighted the need for a concise summary of the wide range of MSME business activities.[1] Across developing Asia, MSMEs are the backbone of domestic demand, job creation, innovation, and competition. A proper summary would be extremely useful when crafting policies to encourage MSME market access, entrepreneurship, use of technology, commercialization, and access to financing. Once MSME activities can be measured using a limited number of meaningful indexes, we can then more easily understand their past and current experience, thus allowing officials to better develop effective MSME policies.

This study follows the 2020 report's recommendations. It reviewed ways of measuring MSME activities as suggested by the Organisation for Economic Co-operation and Development (OECD), the Association of Southeast Asian Nations (ASEAN), the International Trade Centre, the International Finance Corporation, and the World Bank. They proposed a qualitative approach or median comparison to assess MSME development nationally and regionally. The 2020 report suggested developing a more quantitative approach, where the purpose of the SME-DI was to summarize various aspects of MSME business activities—such as sales, employment, exports, imports, and financing. The report proposed a set of potentially useful methods, some of which were tried as a form of test run.

However, despite the need for a solid real data evaluation of MSME development, accurately measuring MSME activities remains at an early stage. Lack of data is the biggest problem. Even in datasets accounting for country-level aggregate variables, missing data entries and/or data series are common. This is more apparent in the case of granular data, for example, firm-level panel data. Second, although research has already proposed a variety of indexes, their practicality leaves them at an early stage of development. Therefore, estimating and interpreting an SME-DI using actual data in various forms is very important, as shown in the ADB 2020 report.

This study first reviews the 2020 SME-DI exercise and defines critical issues. It then proposes using a variant of a principal component analysis (PCA) that can be done practically. After describing the data to be analyzed, the study estimates the SME-DI using the proposed method and interprets its results.

---

[1] ADB. 2020. Asia Small and Medium-Sized Enterprise Monitor 2020. Volume IV–Technical Note: Designing a Small and Medium-Sized Enterprise Development Index.

Lessons from the 2020 SME-DI Exercise

The 2020 ASM offered several possible SME-DI models with test runs. It estimated a pilot regional index for 10 Southeast Asian countries.[2] It also constructed a pilot country index for Cambodia. This section summarizes the tests and lists some practical issues to resolve before upgrading the SME-DI.

For the test runs, the initial exercise considered two sets of data under a framework of a two-stage PCA. The first dataset was aggregate MSME data from the 2020 ASM database. The second was granular company data for Cambodia provided by Credit Bureau Cambodia (CBC). First, various raw data series were categorized into several groups such as macro conditions, bank financing, and nonbank financing, based on the available data. Using a standard PCA, the raw data series were summarized as multiple factors that led to first-stage subindexes. The second stage treated those subindexes as a set of raw data series and processed them again using the PCA. This led to a single SME-DI (second-stage result). The two-stage PCA method is a nested application of a simple PCA with a discretionary categorization of original data series to more easily interpret results.

The pilot testing of the regional SME-DI based on aggregate MSME data was computed addressing either three (macro, bank, nonbank) or four (plus equity) dimensions. The estimates showed that macro conditions were the most significant to MSME development. Meanwhile, MSME financing remained important with the weights for bank and nonbank financing almost equal. The pilot testing of the country SME-DI based on the granular company data from CBC was computed as a finance subindex. The estimates showed that—in terms of financial access, products, and soundness—loans from state-owned banks and US dollar-denominated loans from private banks positively affected MSME financial depth. On the other hand, the nonbank finance industry represented by microfinance institutions (MFIs) contributed less to MSME access to finance in Cambodia.

While the test runs were an important first step in constructing an SME-DI, several issues need to be resolved. First, the two-stage approach for constructing the sub- and main SME-DIs inevitably requires a discretionary categorization of raw variables due to the limited data availability, making it difficult to interpret the results. To enhance the accuracy of the estimates, an analytical model without discretionary categorization should be developed, focusing on non-arbitrary descriptions of data as much as possible. Second, the initial exercise lacked an explicit time-series dimension for analysis. Due to the limited data availability, the two-stage PCA method was applied to the pooled sample both in terms of a cross-section and time series. As the purpose of the index is to easily monitor MSME activities over the years, the pooled sample in the PCA makes understanding the results less straightforward.

Thus, the data limitation issue cannot be overemphasized. The 2020 ASM concluded: "Notable challenges to the SME-DI design were data availability and consistency. Southeast Asia has relatively better data availability on MSMEs than other regions within developing Asia. Nevertheless, more data are needed to correctly estimate an SME-DI. Further efforts are required to obtain country data through (i) extended data-sharing agreements

---

[2] Brunei Darussalam, Cambodia, Indonesia, the Lao PDR, Malaysia, Myanmar, the Philippines, Singapore, Thailand, and Viet Nam.

with public and private sector institutions that hold MSME data, including statistics offices, business registration offices, credit bureaus, government authorities, financial authorities, and central banks; and (ii) dedicated national firm-level surveys to collect missing data." Thus, the second-phase study addresses how to deal with these data limitations, especially missing data.

One obvious approach is to increase the available data provided by each country. However, the current status of data availability is neither complete nor in most cases comparable, even for country-level aggregate variables. Some countries have a nearly full set of aggregate variables regarding MSME activities over extended periods, while other countries are limited in both the number of variables available and the length of time series. If we try to extend the data source from aggregate to granular data (for example, regional-, firm-, or individual-levels), the limitations become even more apparent. Thus, the research should focus on how to deal with datasets with some missing values. Although using data series with no observations is impossible, some recent advances in econometrics allows us to interpolate some missing values in data series systematically.

Another Trial: How to Cope with the Data Limitation

Based on lessons learned from the 2020 SME-DI exercise, we developed a new trial that can deal with these data limitations. The method is a variant of a standard PCA that allows for some missing data. This section provides a detailed explanation of the method used in this study.

1.   Introduction of Probabilistic PCA

The probabilistic PCA in Tipping and Bishop (1999) assumes that every observed data $x \in \mathbb{R}^d$ correspond to a latent variable $z \in \mathbb{R}^{d'}$ and are generated by the following linear model:[3]

$$x = Wz + \mu + \epsilon, \tag{1}$$

where matrix $W \in \mathbb{R}^{d \times d'}$ relates the latent variable to the observed data, μ ($\in \mathbb{R}^d$) is the mean of this model, and ε is the noise. The distribution of z is the k-dimensional standard Gaussian $N(0, I)$, while ϵ comes from the Gaussian $N(0, \sigma^2 I)$. When we have n observed data $\{x_i\}_{i=1}^{n}$, the latent variable and a noise corresponding to x_i are written as z_i and ϵ_i, respectively. We write $X = (x_1, x_2 \cdots, x_n)^T \in \mathbb{R}^{n \times d}$ and $Z = (z_1, z_2 \cdots, z_n)^T \in \mathbb{R}^{n \times d'}$ for simplicity, and each x_i is regarded as identically and independently sampled from the model (1). Thus, model (1) assumes the observed data is realized by the low dimensional ($d' < d$) latent variable. Our goal is to find optimal parameters (μ, W, σ^2) to maximize the posterior likelihood. Before applying the analysis, we regularize X into mean 0 and variance 1 with regard to each column.

Under these premises, the observed variable s_i follows its marginal distribution $x_i \sim N(\mu, WW^T + \sigma^2 I)$ (independent and identically). Thus, we get the following log likelihood function where X is regularized as the zero-mean in the following transformation:

$$\mathcal{L} = \sum_{i=1}^{n} -\frac{1}{2} \left[\log \det \left(WW^\top + \sigma^2 I \right) + (x_i - \mu)^\top \left(WW^\top + \sigma^2 I \right)^{-1} (x_i - \mu) \right]$$

$$= -\frac{1}{2} \left[n \log \det \left(WW^\top + \sigma^2 I \right) - n\mu^\top \left(WW^\top + \sigma^2 I \right)^{-1} \mu + \sum_{i=1}^{n} x_i^\top \left(WW^\top + \sigma^2 I \right)^{-1} x_i \right], \tag{2}$$

where we omitted the independent terms for the maximum likelihood estimation.

According to Tipping and Bishop (1999), the optimal parameters that attain the maximal of L can be explicitly written. Here, we use the eigenvalue decomposition of the covariance matrix of X. Let $(v_1, \lambda 1), \cdots, (v_d, \lambda_d)$ be sets of eigenvector and eigenvalue of $X^T X$ sorted in order of increasing eigenvalues. We set $U = (v_1, \cdots, v_d)$ and $\Lambda = (\lambda_1, \cdots, \lambda_d)$. Using these notations, we have the following solution for the maximum likelihood estimation:

---

[3]   See also Bishop (2006) and Hastie et al. (2009).

$$\begin{cases} \mu_* = 0 \\ W_* = U(\Lambda - \sigma_*^2 I)^{\frac{1}{2}} R \quad \left(R \; (\in \mathbb{R}^{d' \times d'}) \text{ is an arbitrary rotation matrix} \right) \\ \sigma_*^2 = \dfrac{1}{d - d'} \displaystyle\sum_{i=d'+1}^{d} \lambda_i. \end{cases} \tag{3}$$

2.   Expectation-Maximization Algorithm for Complete Data

Apart from the explicit solution to equation (3), there are several useful iterative algorithms to solve optimization problems. The gradient descent method is probably the most popular algorithm for optimization. Here we introduce the expectation-maximization (EM) algorithm which assures that L does not decrease in each step.

In the following exposition, we denote a set of parameters (μ, W, σ^2) as θ. We also subscript the parameters of the k-th iteration as $\theta_k (k = 1, 2, \cdots)$. However, we consider a more generalized setting where the random variables x and z follow a joint distribution $p(x, z|\theta)$ but only x can be observed. We draw n data $\{x_i\}_{i=1}^{n}$ identically and independently from $p(x, z|\theta)$. To apply the maximum likelihood estimation to derive θ_k, the objective function can be written as follows:

$$\begin{aligned} \mathcal{L}(\theta) &= \log p(X|\theta) \\ &= \int p(Z|X, \theta_k) \log p(X|\theta) \, dZ \\ &= \int p(Z|X, \theta_k) \log \frac{p(X, Z|\theta)}{p(Z|X, \theta_k)} \, dZ + \int \log p(Z|X, \theta_k) \, \log \frac{p(Z|X, \theta_k)}{p(Z|X, \theta)} \, dZ \\ &= \int p(Z|X, \theta_k) \log \frac{p(X, Z|\theta)}{p(Z|X, \theta_k)} \, dZ + \mathrm{KL} \left(p(Z|X, \theta_k) \parallel p(Z|X, \theta) \right). \end{aligned}$$

The EM algorithm aims to maximize the first term so that the following equation holds:

$$\theta_{k+1} = \arg\min_{\theta} \int p(Z|X, \theta_k) \log \frac{p(X, Z|\theta)}{p(Z|X, \theta_k)} \, dZ = \arg\min_{\theta} \int p(Z|X, \theta_k) \log p(X, Z|\theta) \, dZ$$

The second term is no less than zero and attains its minimum at $\theta = \theta_k$. Thus, the EM algorithm assures that $L(\theta_{k+1}) \geq L(\theta_k)$ holds for all $k = 1, 2, \cdots$ as follows:

$$Q_k(\theta) = \int p(Z|X, \theta_k) \log p(X, Z|\theta) \, dZ = \sum_{i=1}^{n} \int p(Z|X, \theta_k) \log p(x_i, z_i|\theta) \, dZ = \sum_{i=1}^{n} \int p(z|x_i, \theta_k) \log p(x_i, z_i|\theta) \, dz.$$

Furthermore, $\int p(Z|X, \theta_k) \log p(X, Z|\theta) d\theta$ can be transformed as follows:

$$Q_k(\theta) = \int p(Z|X, \theta_k) \log p(X, Z|\theta) \, dZ = \sum_{i=1}^{n} \int p(Z|X, \theta_k) \log p(x_i, z_i|\theta) \, dZ = \sum_{i=1}^{n} \int p(z|x_i, \theta_k) \log p(x_i, z_i|\theta) \, dz.$$

The second equality holds as (x_i, z_i) $(i = 1, \cdots, n)$ is independent.

In summary, the EM algorithm alternately repeats two steps: an expectation step for $\log p(X, Z|\theta)$ with regard to $p(Z|X, \theta_k$ and to calculate the k-th target function $Q_k(\theta)$, and a maximization step to maximize it. Although there is no guarantee of obtaining a global optimal solution, convergence of its likelihood is guaranteed by its derivation. This method is particularly useful for estimating parameters in latent variable models where the optimization of simultaneous distributions is difficult.

We consider applying the EM algorithm to the probabilistic PCA model. The simultaneous distributions can be written as follows:

$$p(x, z | \mu, W, \sigma^2) = \frac{1}{\sqrt{(2\pi\sigma^2)^d}} \exp\left(-\frac{\|x - Wz - \mu\|_2^2}{2\sigma^2}\right) \cdot \frac{1}{\sqrt{(2\pi)^d}} \exp\left(-\frac{\|z\|_2^2}{2}\right).$$

Then, the conditional distribution $p(z|x_i, \theta_k)$ of z with k-th parameters is given by the following:

$$p(z|x_i, \theta_k) \propto \exp\left(-\frac{1}{2\sigma_k^2}\left(z^\top (W_k^\top W_k + \sigma^2 I)z - 2(x_i - \mu_k)^\top W_k z\right)\right)$$

$$\therefore z|x_i, \theta_k \sim \mathcal{N}\left((W_k^\top W_k + \sigma_k^2 I)^{-1} W_k^\top (x_i - \mu_k), \sigma_k^2 (W_k^\top W_k + \sigma_k^2 I)^{-1}\right)$$

This object means that the mean $<z_i>$ and the covariance $<z_i z_i^T>$ of z under $p(z|x_i, \theta_k)$ can be written respectively as follows, where we denote $(W_k^T W_k + \sigma^2 I)^{-1}$ as M_k:

$$<z_i> = M_k W_k^\top (x_i - \mu_k), \quad <z_i z_i^\top> = \sigma_k^2 M_k + <z_i><z_i>^\top$$

By extracting terms which relate to θ from Q_k, we get the k-th target function:

$$\sum_{i=1}^{n} \int p(z|x_i, \theta_k) \log p(x_i, z_i|\theta)\, dz - (\text{irrelevant terms})$$

$$= \frac{1}{2}\sum_{i=1}^{n} \int p(z|x_i, \theta_k)\left[\log \sigma^2 + z^\top z + \frac{1}{\sigma^2}\left\{(x_i - \mu)^\top (x_i - \mu) - 2(x_i - \mu)^\top W z + z_i^\top W^\top W z_i\right\}\right] dz$$

$$= \frac{1}{2}\left[\log \sigma^2 + \mathrm{tr}(<z_i z_i^\top>) + \frac{1}{\sigma^2}\left\{(x_i - \mu)^\top (x_i - \mu) - 2(x_i - \mu)^\top W<z_i> + \mathrm{tr}(W^\top W<z_i z_i^\top>)\right\}\right].$$

Finally, $\theta_{(k+1)}$ is calculated by differentiating the target function by (μ, W, σ^2) and finding a unique stationary point:

$$\begin{cases} \mu_{k+1} = 0 \\[2mm] W_{k+1} = \left(\sum_{i=1}^{n} x_i <z_i>^\top\right) \cdot \left(\sum_{i=1}^{n} <z_i z_i^\top>\right)^{-1} \\[2mm] \sigma_{k+1}^2 = \frac{1}{n}\sum_{i=1}^{n} \left(\|x_i\|_2^2 - 2x_i^\top W_{k+1} <z_i> + \mathrm{tr}(W_{k+1}^\top W_{k+1} <z_i z_i^\top>)\right) \end{cases},$$

under the condition $\mu_0 = 0$.[4]

3.   Expectation-Maximization Algorithm for Incomplete Data

When the set of data X is missing some values, we decompose each x_i into the following two terms for easier explanation:

$$x_i = I_i^s s_i + I_i^t t_i.$$

---

[4]   The EM algorithm for complete data is summarized in Appendix 1A.

The two variables s_i and t_i correspond to the observed coordinates and missing coordinates, respectively. When x_i consists of u observed coordinates and v missing coordinates, (s_j) is the j-th observed coordinates of x_i, and (t_j) is the j-th missing coordinates of x_i. Therefore, s_i and t_i are u-dimensional and v-dimensional, while $I_i^s (\in \mathbb{R}^{d \times u})$ and $I_i^t (\in \mathbb{R}^{d \times v})$ are defined as follows:

$$(I_i^s)_{lj} = \begin{cases} 1 & (\text{if } j\text{--th observed coordinate of } x_i \text{ is } x_l) \\ 0 & (\text{otherwise}), \end{cases}$$

$$(I_i^t)_{lj} = \begin{cases} 1 & (\text{if } j\text{--th missing coordinate of } x_i \text{ is } x_l) \\ 0 & (\text{otherwise}). \end{cases}$$

Then, the simultaneous distribution of s, t, z under fixed I^s and I^t can be written as follows:

$$p(s,t,z|\mu,W,\sigma^2) = \frac{1}{\sqrt{(2\pi\sigma^2)^d}} \exp\left(-\frac{\|I^s s + I^t t - Wz - \mu\|_2^2}{2\sigma^2}\right) \cdot \frac{1}{\sqrt{(2\pi)^k}} \exp\left(-\frac{\|z\|_2^2}{2}\right).$$

Also, we have conditional distributions about z and t under the observed s.

$$p(t,z|s,\mu,W,\sigma^2) \propto \exp\left(-\frac{1}{2\sigma^2}\begin{bmatrix} z^\top & t^\top \end{bmatrix} \underbrace{\begin{bmatrix} W^\top W + \sigma^2 I & -W^\top I^t \\ -(I^t)^\top & I \end{bmatrix}}_{=:D} \begin{bmatrix} z \\ t \end{bmatrix} + \frac{1}{\sigma^2} \underbrace{\left(\begin{bmatrix} W^\top \\ -(I^t)^\top \end{bmatrix}(I^s s - \mu)\right)^\top}_{=:m} \begin{bmatrix} z \\ t \end{bmatrix}\right).$$

We define and calculate m and D with the mean and variance of t and z under the fixed s. Using these distribution functions, we can derive the EM algorithm for data with missing values by regarding both t and z as latent variables.[5]

---

[5]   The EM algorithm for incomplete data is summarized in Appendix 1B.

Dataset

This section describes the two sets of data we use for estimating the SME-DI. The first dataset comprises the SME-related aggregate variables for 15 countries—10 Southeast Asian countries (Brunei Darussalam, Cambodia, Indonesia, the Lao PDR, Malaysia, Myanmar, the Philippines, Singapore, Thailand, and Viet Nam) and five South Asian countries (Bangladesh, India, Nepal, Pakistan, and Sri Lanka). Using these country-level panel subsets, we construct a regional SME-DI. The second dataset holds Viet Nam firm-level data consisting of variables measuring basic activities. Using this single country firm-level dataset, we construct Viet Nam's SME-DI.[6]

1. Data for Regional SME-DI

The first subsets come from the ASM 2021 database (ADB 2021a and 2021b). It stores many MSME-related variables measured for each country and year. The data cover the years from 2009 to 2020.

Among the various data series in the database, we chose those closely related to MSME activities. The first variable is "number of MSMEs," which is the number of enterprises meeting the MSME criteria for each country and year. It should be noted that MSME definitions differ slightly among designated countries. This study uses national MSME definitions and the number provided by national statistics agencies. The second variable is "number of employees in MSMEs," which measures the number of workers employed by the MSMEs in each country and year. Third, "gross domestic product (GDP) of MSMEs" measures the sum of value-added produced by MSMEs in each country and year. The fourth variable "export from MSMEs" is the value of products exported by MSMEs in each country and year. The fifth to eighth variables measure the status of corporate financing in each country and year. "Bank loan for MSMEs" and "nonperforming loans by MSMEs" correspond to the outstanding amounts of bank loans to MSMEs and the amount of nonperforming loans. "Nonbank loan" and "nonperforming nonbank loan" account for the same sets of variables for loans from nonbank finance institutions available for MSMEs. The final variable "market capitalization" accounts for the market value of listed companies on dedicated MSME market boards or equity markets that MSMEs can tap in each country and year. It should be noted that data include primary market data if MSME market data is unavailable. We add this variable nonetheless to account for the status of the equity market—given that equity financing is one of the important external financing sources for MSMEs. As such a number does not exist for unlisted firms, we represent it by referring to market capitalization.

Table 1 summarizes each variable for each country. It shows that the number of available variables varies by country. This reflects the fact that even country-level aggregate variables are not available for all countries. Among the nine variables listed above, some selected countries such as Indonesia and Thailand include at most seven variables.

---

[6] In addition to these two datasets, we originally planned to use Cambodian firm-level data provided by the Credit Bureau Cambodia (CBC). Due to the COVID-19 pandemic, it was originally planned to do the data analysis through virtual data sharing provided by CBC. But we were unable to complete the analysis remotely. Given these technical difficulties, we decided to use the two datasets presented above.

Table 1: MSME-Related Variables, 2009–2020

Country	Variables	Unit	Obs	Mean	Median	S.D.	Min	Max
Bangladesh	Bank loans for MSMEs	$ million	11	17,995	18,260	5,719	9,478	26,802
	Nonbank loans	$ million	9	6,292	6,743	1,592	3,364	7,912
	Nonperforming nonbank loans	$ million	9	533	510	295	174	1,186
	Market capitalization	$ million	12	37,501	37,966	7,707	17,921	47,093
Brunei Darussalam	GDP of MSMEs	$ million	9	3,235	3,139	538	2,503	3,982
	Nonbank loans	$ million	11	1,252	1,180	139	1,095	1,531
	Nonperforming nonbank loans	$ million	11	15	14	4	10	26
Cambodia	Nonbank loans	$ million	11	3,257	3,107	2,455	299	7,475
	Nonperforming nonbank loans	$ million	12	39	18	41	1	138
	Market capitalization	$ million	9	515	199	692	117	2,411
India	Number of MSMEs		10	46,716,667	45,759,000	7,122,350	37,736,000	63,387,673
	Number of employees in MSMEs		10	101,906,500	103,654,500	10,670,598	84,200,000	117,132,000
	GDP of MSMEs	$ million	11	526,508	548,873	57,439	445,640	615,535
	Export from MSMEs	$ million	8	141,176	137,982	10,691	127,992	159,180
	Bank loans for MSMEs	$ million	12	111,829	93,336	109,777	1,707	255,983
	Market capitalization	$ million	9	1,958	2,574	1,101	52	3,375
Indonesia	Number of MSMEs		10	59,001,245	58,579,247	4,191,630	52,764,750	65,465,497
	Number of employees in MSMEs		10	110,698,728	113,486,346	8,830,419	96,193,623	123,229,386
	GDP of MSMEs	$ million	10	482,190	449,210	105,298	330,258	689,214
	Export from MSMEs	$ million	10	18,456	19,186	3,430	13,481	24,400
	Bank loans for MSMEs	$ million	10	63,553	62,571	10,186	49,949	79,947
	Nonperforming loans by MSMEs	$ million	10	2,392	2,494	494	1,601	3,056
	Market capitalization	$ million	12	413,585	423,522	84,832	214,827	522,625
Lao PDR	Nonbank loans	$ million	11	229	103	247	6	686
	Market capitalization	$ million	10	1,127	1,128	254	578	1,479
Malaysia	GDP of MSMEs	$ million	12	110,815	110,436	14,883	80,398	135,237
	Export from MSMEs	$ million	11	39,058	41,234	4,390	29,355	44,045
	Bank loans for MSMEs	$ million	12	64,409	68,729	11,719	40,178	76,019
	Nonperforming loans by MSMEs	$ million	12	2,598	2,533	317	2,139	3,288
	Nonbank loans	$ million	12	321,298	329,680	135,386	83,215	612,455
	Market capitalization	$ million	12	3,226	2,764	1,887	1,546	8,869
Myanmar	Number of MSMEs		11	49,288	39,272	13,948	38,590	75,116
	Nonbank loans	$ million	8	326	161	369	58	1,228
	Nonperforming nonbank loans	$ million	8	2	1	3	0	10
Nepal	Number of MSMEs		12	248,979	235,538	71,928	156,343	390,493
	Number of employees in MSMEs		12	2,235,325	2,157,744	284,895	1,843,908	2,808,052
	Market capitalization	$ million	12	10,189	9,914	4,971	3,783	18,036
Pakistan	GDP of MSMEs	$ million	12	3,104	3,409	794	1,732	4,139
	Bank loans for MSMEs	$ million	12	3,344	3,176	533	2,579	4,132
	Nonperforming loans by MSMEs	$ million	12	781	778	209	510	1,133
	Nonbank loans	$ million	12	583	560	173	367	820
	Nonperforming nonbank loans	$ million	12	36	31	32	14	137
	Market capitalization	$ million	12	55,779	52,935	17,819	32,112	91,864

continued on next page

Table 1   *continued*

Country	Variables	Unit	Obs	Mean	Median	S.D.	Min	Max
Philippines	Number of MSMEs		12	909,166	929,002	76,564	774,664	998,342
	Number of employees in MSMEs		12	4,744,244	4,885,508	694,882	3,532,935	5,714,262
	Bank loans for MSMEs	$ million	12	9,309	9,658	1,641	5,563	11,604
	Nonperforming loans by MSMEs	$ million	12	581	570	57	521	728
	Nonbank loans	$ million	12	4,420	3,897	4,189	136	12,024
	Market capitalization	$ million	12	322	221	364	7	1,216
Singapore	Bank loans for MSMEs	$ million	12	54,171	53,919	8,598	36,057	68,398
	Nonperforming loans by MSMEs	$ million	12	1,541	1,031	1,107	443	3,126
	Nonbank loans	$ million	12	9,118	9,372	1,284	6,259	10,921
	Market capitalization	$ million	12	6,668	7,008	1,690	3,795	9,591
Sri Lanka	Nonbank loans	$ million	12	9,959	10,709	3,504	3,731	14,506
	Nonperforming nonbank loans	$ million	12	736	666	446	106	1,734
	Market capitalization	$ million	12	17,775	18,570	3,329	9,548	23,692
Thailand	Number of MSMEs		12	2,901,831	2,904,637	162,621	2,646,549	3,134,442
	Number of employees in MSMEs		12	11,601,250	11,580,898	1,168,270	9,701,354	13,950,241
	GDP of MSMEs	$ million	12	165,684	158,676	27,483	115,792	216,148
	Export from MSMEs	$ million	12	54,531	56,839	12,270	27,957	71,675
	Bank loans for MSMEs	$ million	12	160,745	168,491	36,046	75,400	211,978
	Nonperforming loans by MSMEs	$ million	12	5,556	5,095	1,318	4,019	7,938
	Market capitalization	$ million	12	6,700	7,278	3,549	1,174	11,872
Viet Nam	Number of MSMEs		12	421,389	393,915	129,169	230,365	651,138
	Number of employees in MSMEs		12	5,242,966	5,321,882	618,463	3,872,711	6,205,320
	Nonbank loans	$ million	12	2,763	2,827	988	1,252	4,212
	Nonperforming nonbank loans	$ million	12	6	0	12	0	31
	Market capitalization	$ million	12	14,587	2,269	17,126	237	43,262

GDP = gross domestic product, Lao PDR = Lao People's Democratic Republic, MSMEs = micro, small, and medium-sized enterprises.
Source: ADB Asia SME Monitor 2021 database.

In addition, the number of observations for each variable varies for each country. For example, for Bangladesh, there are only nine observations for nonbank loans while market capitalization is recorded 12 times. This difference means certain variables suffer from missing values. Table 2 depicts the pattern of this missing data. For example, while a large number are observed for the first several years and the very end of the sample period, the GDP of MSMEs for Brunei Darussalam is missing for 2014. These facts motivate use to apply the method introduced in the previous section.

Table 2: Missing Data

Country	Variables	2009	2010	2011	2012	2013	2014	2015	2016	2017	2018	2019	2020
Bangladesh	Bank loans for MSMEs	NA											
	Nonbank loans	NA	NA	NA									
	Nonperforming nonbank loans	NA	NA	NA									
	Market capitalization												
Brunei Darussalam	GDP of MSMEs	NA					NA						NA
	Nonbank loans	NA											
	Nonperforming nonbank loans	NA											
Cambodia	Nonbank loans		NA										
	Nonperforming nonbank loans												
	Market capitalization	NA	NA	NA									
India	Number of MSMEs											NA	NA
	Number of employees in MSMEs											NA	NA
	GDP of MSMEs												NA
	Export from MSMEs	NA	NA	NA	NA								
	Bank loans for MSMEs												
	Market capitalization	NA	NA	NA									
Indonesia	Number of MSMEs	NA											NA
	Number of employees in MSMEs	NA											NA
	GDP of MSMEs	NA											NA
	Export from MSMEs	NA											NA
	Bank loans for MSMEs	NA	NA										
	Nonperforming loans by MSMEs	NA	NA										
	Market capitalization												
Lao PDR	Nonbank loans	NA											
	Market capitalization	NA	NA										
Malaysia	GDP of MSMEs												
	Export from MSMEs	NA											
	Bank loans for MSMEs												
	Nonperforming loans by MSMEs												
	Nonbank loans												
	Market capitalization												
Myanmar	Number of MSMEs												NA
	Nonbank loans	NA	NA	NA									NA
	Nonperforming nonbank loans	NA	NA	NA									NA
Nepal	Number of MSMEs	NA											NA
	Number of employees in MSMEs												NA
	Market capitalization												
Pakistan	GDP of MSMEs												
	Bank loans for MSMEs												
	Nonperforming loans by MSMEs												
	Nonbank loans												
	Nonperforming nonbank loans												
	Market capitalization												

continued on next page

Table 2   *continued*

Country	Variables	2009	2010	2011	2012	2013	2014	2015	2016	2017	2018	2019	2020
Philippines	Number of MSMEs												
	Number of employees in MSMEs												
	Bank loans for MSMEs												
	Nonperforming loans by MSMEs	NA											
	Nonbank loans												
	Market capitalization												
Singapore	Bank loans for MSMEs	NA											
	Nonperforming loans by MSMEs	NA											
	Nonbank loans	NA											
	Market capitalization												
Sri Lanka	Nonbank loans												
	Nonperforming nonbank loans												
	Market capitalization												
Thailand	Number of MSMEs												
	Number of employees in MSMEs												
	GDP of MSMEs												
	Export from MSMEs												
	Bank loans for MSMEs												
	Nonperforming loans by MSMEs												
	Market capitalization												
Viet Nam	Number of MSMEs												NA
	Number of employees in MSMEs												NA
	Nonbank loans	NA											
	Nonperforming nonbank loans	NA	NA										
	Market capitalization												

GDP = gross domestic product, Lao PDR = Lao People's Democratic Republic, MSMEs = micro, small, and medium-sized enterprises.
Source: ADB Asia SME Monitor 2021 database.

2.   Data for Country SME-DI: Viet Nam

The second MSME dataset comes from 2017–2019 enterprise registration data obtained from the Agency for Business Registration (ABR) in Viet Nam. The number of samples was 4,785 MSMEs. The data store firm-level variables measured for each firm and year. For this study, we gained access to registered enterprise data recorded over the 3 years. Table 3A summarizes the firm-level data. In addition to a summary of data pooled for all industries, we also break down data by industry, as we will use the industry and year-level panel data for estimating the SME-DI for Viet Nam.

From the firm-level information registered by the ABR, we exclude data recorded as "large" so we can focus on MSMEs. Of the information available, we chose three variables to measure MSME activities. The first is "total employees," which measures the number of workers employed by each firm in each year. Second, "revenue" measures each firm's sales in each year. The third, "profit," is the net profit of each firm in each year. The last two variables are measured in Vietnamese dong.

Given that the 3-year time series is much smaller than the number of firms, we summarize the firm-level data by industry and year. Table 3B summarizes the industry-level panel data. Similar to Table 3A, in addition to the data summary pooled for all industries, we show the summary for each industry. These industry and year-level panel data are used to estimate the SME-DI for Viet Nam.

One important difference between Viet Nam's firm-level (industry-level) data and the Asian country-level panel data is that Viet Nam is not missing any data. As shown in Table 3B, each variable for each industry has three records corresponding to the three ABR data from 2017 to 2019. This means we do not need to use a probabilistic PCA but rather the standard PCA.

Table 3: MSME-Related Variables—Viet Nam, 2017-2019

A. Firm-Level Panel Data

Industry	Variables	Obs	Mean	Median	S.D.	Min	Max
ALL	Total employees	4,219	13	9	21	1	307
	Revenue	4,428	415,330,476,564	6,658,995,624	4,268,606,405,364	−882,237,503	153,923,084,501,219
	Profit	4,488	11,614,166,901	14,114,349	212,837,537,694	−1,466,008,986,437	7,405,418,331,836
Manufacturing	Total employees	237	13	9	15	2	87
	Revenue	237	22,575,189,319	6,124,148,600	43,826,687,556	0	299,289,199,551
	Profit	238	91,801,467	9,231,512	1,535,806,246	−6,306,997,797	21,634,942,603
Wholesale and retail trade	Total employees	922	12	8	20	2	164
	Revenue	918	42,650,911,962	10,496,098,814	139,661,596,801	0	2,182,645,170,718
	Profit	924	116,365,474	25,758,373	4,932,364,599	−109,089,509,500	51,426,967,033
Agri-food services	Total employees	153	17	6	22	3	125
	Revenue	148	36,843,497,128	7,856,775,084	71,955,807,360	0	386,783,422,448
	Profit	150	124,046,616	16,389,075	1,722,442,897	−6,792,816,882	14,037,420,653
Construction	Total employees	438	14	10	24	2	307
	Revenue	431	42,006,482,634	6,510,739,800	119,800,987,245	0	1,163,356,189,300
	Profit	437	434,814,954	11,185,388	5,553,226,576	−36,665,925,498	67,145,316,200
Transportation	Total employees	124	12	7	16	3	90
	Revenue	121	54,515,824,675	11,754,402,989	130,882,198,856	0	932,141,356,200
	Profit	122	268,408,066	26,298,858	1,194,170,195	−1,866,892,170	7,348,160,728
Other services	Total employees	521	13	10	20	2	190
	Revenue	515	20,423,923,624	4,043,546,500	49,750,830,340	0	552,528,210,953
	Profit	524	211,403,872	16,788,996	2,598,236,070	−18,581,347,291	23,097,913,454
Others	Total employees	308	18	10	31	2	197
	Revenue	304	17,441,685,260	3,983,982,718	47,108,042,737	0	533,969,045,165
	Profit	308	378,353,162	12,415,555	3,086,020,055	−1,561,425,015	48,791,352,211

B. Industry-Level Panel Data

Industry	Variables	Obs	Mean	Median	S.D.	Min	Max
ALL	Total employees	3	18,771	18,871	1,590	17,133	20,308
	Revenue	3	613,027,783,408,415	568,944,324,767,529	108,065,754,049,532	533,972,066,153,848	736,166,959,303,867
	Profit	3	17,374,793,683,906	18,479,396,491,751	2,884,880,653,183	14,100,833,620,125	19,544,150,939,842
Manufacturing	Total employees	3	1,044	1,087	239	787	1,259
	Revenue	3	1,783,439,956,185	1,798,255,584,381	564,413,603,721	1,211,764,396,300	2,340,299,887,875
	Profit	3	7,282,916,346	4,286,900,600	11,196,928,006	−2,111,234,153	19,673,082,592

continued on next page

Table 3   *continued*

Industry	Variables	Obs	Mean	Median	S.D.	Min	Max
Wholesale and retail trade	Total employees	3	3,795	3,807	615	3,174	4,404
	Revenue	3	13,051,179,060,437	13,143,589,791,291	3,171,955,785,529	9,834,027,669,300	16,175,919,720,720
	Profit	3	35,840,565,969	87,195,648,919	164,812,787,061	−148,535,577,800	168,861,626,789
Agri-food services	Total employees	3	855	847	143	716	1,002
	Revenue	3	1,817,612,524,988	1,861,914,961,214	324,589,274,309	1,473,147,534,900	2,117,775,078,849
	Profit	3	6,202,330,796	6,336,117,589	4,727,712,545	1,409,144,800	10,861,729,998
Construction	Total employees	3	2,077	2,138	442	1,608	2,485
	Revenue	3	6,034,931,338,465	6,587,528,159,413	1,340,280,071,763	4,506,703,123,300	7,010,562,732,681
	Profit	3	63,338,044,970	67,343,786,400	24,576,291,812	37,004,953,419	85,665,395,090
Transportation	Total employees	3	496	507	65	426	554
	Revenue	3	2,198,804,928,576	2,211,986,375,584	221,500,304,220	1,971,008,256,100	2,413,420,154,044
	Profit	3	10,915,261,349	12,073,736,614	3,072,818,862	7,431,601,734	13,240,445,700
Other services	Total employees	3	2,328	2,410	442	1,850	2,723
	Revenue	3	3,506,106,888,833	3,285,781,176,186	1,029,914,841,060	2,604,184,267,000	4,628,355,223,313
	Profit	3	36,925,209,707	53,414,095,623	30,672,430,787	1,535,131,900	55,826,401,597
Others	Total employees	3	1,810	1,849	261	1,532	2,049
	Revenue	3	1,767,424,106,346	1,654,328,190,053	775,396,602,294	1,054,786,211,700	2,593,157,917,286
	Profit	3	38,844,257,921	30,961,680,386	32,585,241,973	10,923,394,800	74,647,698,578

MSME = micro, small, and medium-sized enterprise.

Source: MSME data from the 2017–2019 Agency for Business Registration, Viet Nam enterprise registration data.

Estimation Results

This section presents the estimation results on the regional SME-DI (i) covering all 15 countries, (ii) for Southeast Asia, and (iii) for South Asia; and the country SME-DI for Viet Nam.

1.   Regional SME-DI: Overall Estimate

The regional SME-DI for 15 Asian countries showed that the 2008–2009 global financial crisis slowed MSME development until 2014, nonperforming MSME loans increased, and the number of MSMEs decreased. But this was followed by a recovery in capital markets and MSME financing between 2013 and 2015, advancing MSME development.

To estimate the regional SME-DI, the probabilistic PCA was applied to the country-level panel data and obtain three factors, principal component (PC)1 to PC3 (Figure 1 and Table 4).

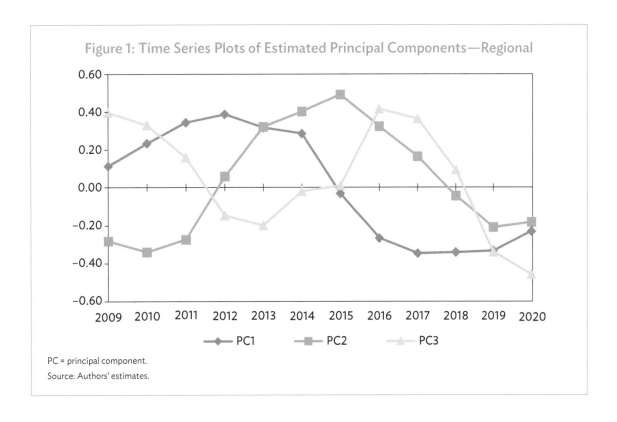

Figure 1: Time Series Plots of Estimated Principal Components—Regional

PC = principal component.

Source: Authors' estimates.

Table 4: Time Series of Estimated Principal Components—Regional

	2009	2010	2011	2012	2013	2014	2015	2016	2017	2018	2019	2020
PC1	0.11	0.23	0.34	0.39	0.32	0.29	-0.03	-0.27	-0.35	-0.34	-0.34	-0.23
PC2	-0.29	-0.34	-0.28	0.06	0.32	0.40	0.49	0.32	0.16	-0.04	-0.21	-0.18
PC3	0.40	0.33	0.16	-0.15	-0.20	-0.02	0.01	0.42	0.36	0.09	-0.34	-0.46

PC = principal component.
Source: Authors' estimates.

First, the three factors show differing time-series dynamics. For example, PC1 remains high over the first half of the 2009–2014 sample period, which corresponds to the aftermath of the 2008–2009 global financial crisis. It goes down afterward. PC2 reaches its peak in the middle of the sample period while PC3 shows more complex dynamics.

Second, PC1 makes the largest contribution to the variation in country-level panel data (33%), followed by PC2 (22%) and PC3 (13%) (Table 5). Given that more than 50% of the variation is explained by the first two factors, we will focus mainly on those in interpreting the results.

Table 5: Contribution of Each Estimated Principal Component (1)

	PC1	PC2	PC3
Eigenvalue	3.92	2.69	1.55
Contribution ratio	0.33	0.22	0.13
Cumulative contribution rate	0.33	0.55	0.68

PC = principal component.
Source: Authors' estimates.

Third, Table 6 lists the loadings of each factor for each variable. We mark the factor loadings with a darker red (blue) color when they are positive and large (negative and small). Given the mechanics of the PCA, each PC has unique patterns of the factor loadings to some extent. To see this more clearly and interpret the implication of each factor, the three columns in Table 7 list the factor loadings sorted in descending order.

By construction, each factor is orthogonal to each other and related to each variable with specific factor loadings (the coefficients associated with the principal components). Examining these, we can interpret the meaning of each factor.

For PC1, we found positive and large factor loadings for variables such as bank nonperforming loans (NPLs) by MSMEs and nonbank NPLs in countries such as Pakistan (bank NPLs=6.52), Malaysia (bank NPLs=5.63), the Philippines (bank NPLs=2.83), and Brunei Darussalam (nonbank NPLs=2.21). Although we simultaneously found negative factor loadings for PC1 for bank NPLs by MSMEs, for example, in Singapore (bank NPLs=–1.79), they are relatively small in absolute value. The results indicate that PC1 mainly accounts for the negative impact associated with the status of corporate financing in the Asian region covering 15 countries. PC1 reached its peak in 2012 and kept positive factor loadings until 2014, while negative factor loadings were identified after 2015 through 2020. This suggests the GFC hurt MSME development until 2014 with increasing nonperforming MSME loans, but MSME loan asset quality gradually improved after 2015 and remained that way through end-2020.

Although absolute values are not necessarily large, we also found that PC1 has negative and small factor loadings associated with the number of MSMEs in Indonesia (–1.83), Myanmar (–1.78), Thailand (–1.72), and Nepal (–1.67).

Table 6: Factor Loadings Based on Probabilistic PCA—Regional

Country	Variables	PC1	PC2	PC3
Bangladesh	Bank loans for MSMEs	-1.56	0.66	-0.45
	Nonbank loans	-1.65	-1.22	0.80
	Nonperforming nonbank loans	-0.56	-1.41	-0.58
	Market capitalization	-0.55	0.52	0.69
Brunei Darussalam	GDP of MSMEs	-0.80	0.02	0.48
	Nonbank loans	5.29	2.82	-1.64
	Nonperforming nonbank loans	2.21	1.03	-1.96
Cambodia	Nonbank loans	-1.31	-0.73	-0.73
	Nonperforming nonbank loans	-1.23	-0.88	0.05
	Market capitalization	1.15	-1.65	-1.20
India	Number of MSMEs	-1.09	0.61	0.16
	Number of employees in MSMEs	-0.34	2.51	0.84
	GDP of MSMEs	0.59	-4.32	1.63
	Export from MSMEs	0.51	-2.35	-1.18
	Bank loans for MSMEs	-1.93	0.08	0.48
	Market capitalization	-1.63	-1.01	1.79
Indonesia	Number of MSMEs	-1.83	0.46	-0.35
	Number of employees in MSMEs	-0.98	2.27	-0.89
	GDP of MSMEs	-1.53	-0.33	-0.79
	Export from MSMEs	-0.17	-3.20	0.79
	Bank loans for MSMEs	-1.34	-1.19	-0.32
	Nonperforming loans by MSMEs	-1.51	0.05	0.38
	Market capitalization	-0.20	-0.47	-0.16
Lao PDR	Nonbank loans	-1.06	-1.42	-0.98
	Market capitalization	0.15	3.87	0.30
Malaysia	GDP of MSMEs	0.36	-0.27	-1.49
	Export from MSMEs	3.90	-0.93	0.19
	Bank loans for MSMEs	0.20	2.41	-0.47
	Nonperforming loans by MSMEs	5.63	-3.37	0.49
	Nonbank loans	3.99	1.01	2.07
	Market capitalization	0.71	-0.86	-1.50
Myanmar	Number of MSMEs	-1.78	-1.28	0.42
	Nonbank loans	-0.62	-1.67	-1.88
	Nonperforming nonbank loans	-0.70	-1.91	-1.66
Nepal	Number of MSMEs	-1.67	-0.16	-0.90
	Number of employees in MSMEs	-1.31	0.05	-0.67
	Market capitalization	-1.91	0.66	1.66
Pakistan	GDP of MSMEs	-1.24	1.68	0.44
	Bank loans for MSMEs	-0.07	-2.25	4.31
	Nonperforming loans by MSMEs	6.52	-1.56	1.55
	Nonbank loans	-2.26	0.34	1.42
	Nonperforming nonbank loans	4.54	0.47	0.16
	Market capitalization	0.08	3.26	1.86
Philippines	Number of MSMEs	0.57	1.10	-1.76
	Number of employees in MSMEs	-0.03	1.06	-1.36
	Bank loans for MSMEs	-0.36	1.16	-0.67
	Nonperforming loans by MSMEs	2.83	-2.03	-2.62
	Nonbank loans	-1.87	0.34	0.74
	Market capitalization	0.80	1.01	-0.39
Singapore	Bank loans for MSMEs	-0.51	1.00	-1.57
	Nonperforming loans by MSMEs	-1.79	-1.13	0.54
	Nonbank loans	0.08	1.34	-2.30
	Market capitalization	-0.08	1.80	-0.20
Sri Lanka	Nonbank loans	-1.33	1.51	0.46
	Nonperforming nonbank loans	-0.47	-0.56	-1.25
	Market capitalization	3.68	1.98	0.68
Thailand	Number of MSMEs	-1.72	-1.62	0.95
	Number of employees in MSMEs	-0.57	-0.51	0.21
	GDP of MSMEs	-1.09	0.08	0.14
	Export from MSMEs	3.30	0.76	2.68
	Bank loans for MSMEs	-0.11	1.36	-0.69
	Nonperforming loans by MSMEs	-1.60	-1.75	0.24
	Market capitalization	-0.15	2.89	0.95
Viet Nam	Number of MSMEs	-1.41	0.25	-0.29
	Number of employees in MSMEs	0.02	2.03	0.26
	Nonbank loans	-1.72	0.73	0.12
	Nonperforming nonbank loans	0.77	-1.71	-2.04
	Market capitalization	-1.39	-1.48	-0.15

GDP = gross domestic product, Lao PDR = Lao People's Democratic Republic, MSMEs = micro, small, and medium-sized enterprises, PCA = principal component analysis.

Source: Authors' estimates.

This result shows that PC1 also accounts for the small presence of MSME activities right after the GFC and during its recovery.

As for PC2, it had positive and large factor loadings for market capitalization in the Lao PDR (3.87), Pakistan (3.26), Thailand (2.89), Sri Lanka (1.98), and Singapore (1.80). These results show that PC2 largely accounts for the recovery in capital markets after the GFC. Data in the Lao PDR, Pakistan, and Sri Lanka used the stock exchange main board data, while those in Thailand and Singapore used data on emerging markets available to MSMEs (mai and Catalist, respectively). Pakistan introduced its Growth Enterprise Market in 2019 to serve growth-oriented firms, including MSMEs, with reduced listing requirements. Sri Lanka launched its Empower Board under the Colombo Stock Exchange in 2018, as a sponsor-driven equity market dedicated to small businesses. However, there were no market data available as of the end of 2021.

Table 7: Descending Order: Factor Loadings Based on Probabilistic PCA—Regional

Country	Variables	PC1	Country	Variables	PC2	Country	Variables	PC3
Pakistan	Nonperforming loans by MSMEs	6.52	Lao PDR	Market capitalization	3.87	Pakistan	Bank loans for MSMEs	4.31
Malaysia	Nonperforming loans by MSMEs	5.63	Pakistan	Market capitalization	3.26	Thailand	Export from MSMEs	2.68
Brunei Darussalam	Nonbank loans	5.29	Thailand	Market capitalization	2.89	Malaysia	Nonbank loans	2.07
Pakistan	Nonperforming nonbank loans	4.54	Brunei Darussalam	Nonbank loans	2.82	Pakistan	Market capitalization	1.86
Malaysia	Nonbank loans	3.99	India	Number of employees in MSMEs	2.51	India	Market capitalization	1.79
Malaysia	Export from MSMEs	3.90	Malaysia	Bank loans for MSMEs	2.41	Nepal	Market capitalization	1.66
Sri Lanka	Market capitalization	3.68	Indonesia	Number of employees in MSMEs	2.27	India	GDP of MSMEs	1.63
Thailand	Export from MSMEs	3.30	Viet Nam	Number of employees in MSMEs	2.03	Pakistan	Nonperforming loans by MSMEs	1.55
Philippines	Nonperforming loans by MSMEs	2.83	Sri Lanka	Market capitalization	1.98	Pakistan	Nonbank loans	1.42
Brunei Darussalam	Nonperforming nonbank loans	2.21	Singapore	Market capitalization	1.80	Thailand	Market capitalization	0.95
Cambodia	Market capitalization	1.15	Pakistan	GDP of MSMEs	1.68	Thailand	Number of MSMEs	0.95
Philippines	Market capitalization	0.80	Sri Lanka	Nonbank loans	1.51	India	Number of employees in MSMEs	0.84
Viet Nam	Nonperforming nonbank loans	0.77	Thailand	Bank loans for MSMEs	1.36	Bangladesh	Nonbank loans	0.80
Malaysia	Market capitalization	0.71	Singapore	Nonbank loans	1.34	Indonesia	Export from MSMEs	0.79
India	GDP of MSMEs	0.59	Philippines	Bank loans for MSMEs	1.16	Philippines	Nonbank loans	0.74
Philippines	Number of MSMEs	0.57	Philippines	Number of MSMEs	1.10	Bangladesh	Market capitalization	0.69
India	Export from MSMEs	0.51	Philippines	Number of employees in MSMEs	1.06	Sri Lanka	Market capitalization	0.68
Malaysia	GDP of MSMEs	0.36	Brunei Darussalam	Nonperforming nonbank loans	1.03	Singapore	Nonperforming loans by MSMEs	0.54
Malaysia	Bank loans for MSMEs	0.20	Malaysia	Nonbank loans	1.01	Malaysia	Nonperforming loans by MSMEs	0.49
Lao PDR	Market capitalization	0.15	Philippines	Market capitalization	1.01	Brunei Darussalam	GDP of MSMEs	0.48
Singapore	Nonbank loans	0.08	Singapore	Bank loans for MSMEs	1.00	India	Bank loans for MSMEs	0.48
Pakistan	Market capitalization	0.08	Thailand	Export from MSMEs	0.76	Sri Lanka	Nonbank loans	0.46
Viet Nam	Number of employees in MSMEs	0.02	Viet Nam	Nonbank loans	0.73	Pakistan	GDP of MSMEs	0.44
Philippines	Number of employees in MSMEs	-0.03	Bangladesh	Bank loans for MSMEs	0.66	Myanmar	Number of MSMEs	0.42
Pakistan	Bank loans for MSMEs	-0.07	Nepal	Market capitalization	0.66	Indonesia	Nonperforming loans by MSMEs	0.38
Singapore	Market capitalization	-0.08	India	Number of MSMEs	0.61	Lao PDR	Market capitalization	0.30
Thailand	Bank loans for MSMEs	-0.11	Bangladesh	Market capitalization	0.52	Viet Nam	Number of employees in MSMEs	0.26
Thailand	Market capitalization	-0.15	Pakistan	Nonperforming nonbank loans	0.47	Thailand	Nonperforming loans by MSMEs	0.24
Indonesia	Export from MSMEs	-0.17	Indonesia	Number of MSMEs	0.46	Thailand	Number of employees in MSMEs	0.21
Indonesia	Market capitalization	-0.20	Pakistan	Nonbank loans	0.34	Malaysia	Export from MSMEs	0.19
India	Number of employees in MSMEs	-0.34	Philippines	Nonbank loans	0.34	India	Number of MSMEs	0.16
Philippines	Bank loans for MSMEs	-0.36	Viet Nam	Number of MSMEs	0.25	Pakistan	Nonperforming nonbank loans	0.16
Sri Lanka	Nonperforming nonbank loans	-0.47	Thailand	GDP of MSMEs	0.08	Thailand	GDP of MSMEs	0.14
Singapore	Bank loans for MSMEs	-0.51	India	Bank loans for MSMEs	0.08	Viet Nam	Nonbank loans	0.12
Bangladesh	Market capitalization	-0.55	Indonesia	Nonperforming loans by MSMEs	0.05	Cambodia	Nonperforming nonbank loans	0.05
Bangladesh	Nonperforming nonbank loans	-0.56	Nepal	Number of employees in MSMEs	0.05	Viet Nam	Market capitalization	-0.15
Thailand	Number of employees in MSMEs	-0.57	Brunei Darussalam	GDP of MSMEs	0.02	Indonesia	Market capitalization	-0.16
Myanmar	Nonbank loans	-0.62	Nepal	Number of MSMEs	-0.16	Singapore	Market capitalization	-0.20
Myanmar	Nonperforming nonbank loans	-0.70	Malaysia	GDP of MSMEs	-0.27	Viet Nam	Number of MSMEs	-0.29
Brunei Darussalam	GDP of MSMEs	-0.80	Indonesia	GDP of MSMEs	-0.33	Indonesia	Bank loans for MSMEs	-0.32
Indonesia	Number of employees in MSMEs	-0.98	Indonesia	Market capitalization	-0.47	Indonesia	Number of MSMEs	-0.35
Lao PDR	Nonbank loans	-1.06	Thailand	Number of employees in MSMEs	-0.51	Philippines	Market capitalization	-0.39
Thailand	GDP of MSMEs	-1.09	Sri Lanka	Nonperforming nonbank loans	-0.56	Bangladesh	Bank loans for MSMEs	-0.45
India	Number of MSMEs	-1.09	Cambodia	Nonbank loans	-0.73	Malaysia	Bank loans for MSMEs	-0.47
Cambodia	Nonperforming nonbank loans	-1.23	Malaysia	Market capitalization	-0.86	Bangladesh	Nonperforming nonbank loans	-0.58
Pakistan	GDP of MSMEs	-1.24	Cambodia	Nonperforming nonbank loans	-0.88	Nepal	Number of employees in MSMEs	-0.67
Nepal	Number of employees in MSMEs	-1.31	Malaysia	Export from MSMEs	-0.93	Philippines	Bank loans for MSMEs	-0.67
Cambodia	Nonbank loans	-1.31	India	Market capitalization	-1.01	Thailand	Bank loans for MSMEs	-0.69
Sri Lanka	Nonbank loans	-1.33	Singapore	Nonperforming loans by MSMEs	-1.13	Cambodia	Nonbank loans	-0.73
Indonesia	Bank loans for MSMEs	-1.34	Indonesia	Bank loans for MSMEs	-1.19	Indonesia	GDP of MSMEs	-0.79
Viet Nam	Market capitalization	-1.39	Bangladesh	Nonbank loans	-1.22	Indonesia	Number of employees in MSMEs	-0.89
Viet Nam	Number of MSMEs	-1.41	Myanmar	Number of MSMEs	-1.28	Nepal	Number of MSMEs	-0.90
Indonesia	Nonperforming loans by MSMEs	-1.51	Bangladesh	Nonperforming nonbank loans	-1.41	Lao PDR	Nonbank loans	-0.98
Indonesia	GDP of MSMEs	-1.53	Lao PDR	Nonbank loans	-1.42	India	Export from MSMEs	-1.18
Bangladesh	Bank loans for MSMEs	-1.56	Viet Nam	Market capitalization	-1.48	Cambodia	Market capitalization	-1.20
Thailand	Nonperforming loans by MSMEs	-1.60	Pakistan	Nonperforming loans by MSMEs	-1.56	Sri Lanka	Nonperforming nonbank loans	-1.25
India	Market capitalization	-1.63	Thailand	Number of MSMEs	-1.62	Philippines	Number of employees in MSMEs	-1.36
Bangladesh	Nonbank loans	-1.65	Cambodia	Market capitalization	-1.65	Malaysia	GDP of MSMEs	-1.49
Nepal	Number of MSMEs	-1.67	Myanmar	Nonbank loans	-1.67	Malaysia	Market capitalization	-1.50
Viet Nam	Nonbank loans	-1.72	Viet Nam	Nonperforming nonbank loans	-1.71	Singapore	Bank loans for MSMEs	-1.57
Thailand	Number of MSMEs	-1.72	Thailand	Nonperforming loans by MSMEs	-1.75	Brunei Darussalam	Nonbank loans	-1.64
Myanmar	Number of MSMEs	-1.78	Myanmar	Nonperforming nonbank loans	-1.91	Myanmar	Nonperforming nonbank loans	-1.66
Singapore	Nonperforming loans by MSMEs	-1.79	Philippines	Nonperforming loans by MSMEs	-2.03	Philippines	Number of MSMEs	-1.76
Indonesia	Number of MSMEs	-1.83	Pakistan	Bank loans for MSMEs	-2.25	Myanmar	Nonbank loans	-1.88
Philippines	Nonbank loans	-1.87	India	Export from MSMEs	-2.35	Brunei Darussalam	Nonperforming nonbank loans	-1.96
Nepal	Market capitalization	-1.91	Indonesia	Export from MSMEs	-3.20	Viet Nam	Nonperforming nonbank loans	-2.04
India	Bank loans for MSMEs	-1.93	Malaysia	Nonperforming loans by MSMEs	-3.37	Singapore	Nonbank loans	-2.30
Pakistan	Nonbank loans	-2.26	India	GDP of MSMEs	-4.32	Philippines	Nonperforming loans by MSMEs	-2.62

GDP = gross domestic product, Lao PDR = Lao People's Democratic Republic, MSMEs = micro, small, and medium-sized enterprises, PCA = principal component analysis.

Source: Authors' estimates.

Somewhat logically, PC2 also had negative and small factor loadings for bank NPLs in Malaysia (–3.37), the Philippines (–2.03), Thailand (–1.75), and for nonbank NPLs in Myanmar (–1.91) and Viet Nam (–1.71). Given that PC2 reached its peak from 2013 to 2015, the recovery of corporate finance, exemplified by smaller defaults in specific countries, was successfully captured by PC2.

As mentioned, PC3 shows relatively complicated dynamics. This is consistent with the fact that PC3 was positively linked to various variables ranging from bank loans for MSMEs in Pakistan (4.31) to market capitalization in Pakistan (1.86), India (1.79), and Nepal (1.66), and are negatively linked to nonbank NPLs in Viet Nam (–2.04), Brunei Darussalam (–1.96), and Myanmar (–1.66) as well as bank NPLs by MSMEs in the Philippines (–2.62). These results indicated PC3 accounts for the recovery in some countries' capital markets and in corporate financing.

We should highlight that these results are obtained from the probabilistic PCA. This means that even when some records in specific data series are missing, we can still obtain reliable PCs. From a practical point of view, this resilience against missing data is highly attractive.

2.   Regional SME-DI: Southeast Asia

In Southeast Asia after the GFC until 2014, Malaysia and the Philippines contributed to region's increased nonperforming MSME loans. The value of MSME exports decreased in Malaysia and Thailand, which also harmed MSME development in the region. From 2013 to 2015, a recovery in capital markets, especially for growth firms including MSMEs on Thailand's mai and Singapore's Catalist, contributed to a recovery of the region's MSME sector. After 2016, MSME development in the region was supported by increased number of MSMEs in Indonesia and Viet Nam; more nonbank loans in Viet Nam, Cambodia, and the Philippines; and higher MSME value-added (GDP) in Indonesia and Thailand.

This subsection describes what occurred in Southeast Asia using subsamples of country-level panel data in 10 countries: Brunei Darussalam, Cambodia, Indonesia, the Lao PDR, Malaysia, Myanmar, the Philippines, Singapore, Thailand, and Viet Nam. Later, we break down the analysis covering South Asian countries of Bangladesh, India, Nepal, Pakistan, and Sri Lanka for comparison.

The analysis attempts to do two things. First, we double-check the robustness of our results presented earlier. As shown in the previous section, we link the dynamics of each factor to a set of variables and factor loadings associated with each country. We predict these will also appear in the analysis of the subsamples. Second, we examine any differences in the dynamics of estimated factors between Southeast Asia and South Asia.

Applying the probabilistic PCA to the subsample in Southeast Asia, we obtained the three PC1 to PC3 factors (Figure 2 and Table 8). As summarized in Table 9, the contribution of the three factors was 83%.

PC1 and PC2 for the Southeast Asian group show highly similar dynamics as the overall estimates of the entire 15 countries. PC1 remains low over the first half of the periods from 2009 to 2014, and then rises afterward. PC2 reaches its peak in the middle of the sample period in 2015. From the results associated with the estimated factor loadings, we confirmed that factors correspond to the PC1 and PC2 as shown in the overall estimates (Table 10). The dynamics of PC1 in this subsample analysis are opposite of those in the overall estimates. This is simply because factor loadings are estimated with opposite signs to those in the overall estimates. It was constructed so the sign of a factor and associated factor loadings are not identifiable without additional restrictions. Thus, we can confirm the exact correspondence between the results we obtained in the overall estimates and this subsample analysis.

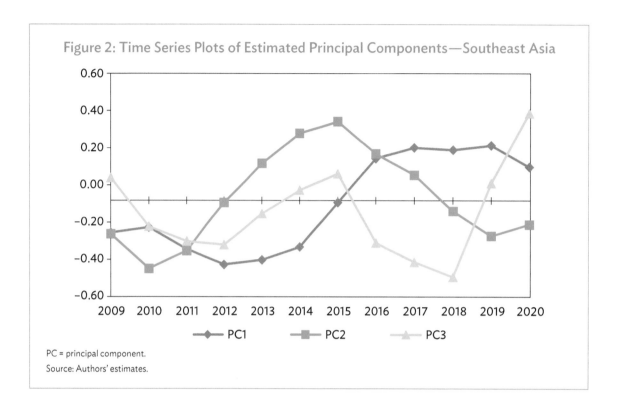

Figure 2: Time Series Plots of Estimated Principal Components—Southeast Asia

PC = principal component.
Source: Authors' estimates.

Table 8: Time Series of Estimated Principal Components—Southeast Asia

	2009	2010	2011	2012	2013	2014	2015	2016	2017	2018	2019	2020
PC1	-0.20	-0.17	-0.31	-0.40	-0.37	-0.29	-0.01	0.26	0.33	0.32	0.35	0.21
PC2	-0.21	-0.43	-0.32	-0.01	0.23	0.42	0.50	0.29	0.16	-0.07	-0.22	-0.15
PC3	0.14	-0.16	-0.26	-0.28	-0.08	0.07	0.17	-0.27	-0.39	-0.48	0.11	0.55

PC = principal component.
Source: Authors' estimates.

Table 9: Contribution of Each Estimated Principal Component (2)

	PC1	PC2	PC3
Eigenvalue	3.86	2.86	1.56
Contribution ratio	0.57	0.18	0.08
Cumulative contribution rate	0.57	0.75	0.83

PC = principal component.
Source: Authors' estimates.

We found a different pattern of PC3 for Southeast Asia from that in the overall estimates, which had relatively complex dynamics. From the estimated factor loadings, however, we found that PC3 for Southeast Asia is largely driven by market capitalization. This is consistent with the fact that the PC3 in the overall estimates also accounted for the recovery in some specific countries' capital markets. Thus, the difference in those two PC3s originates from the difference in the timing of recovery, but not from the types of variables behind the factor dynamics.

When examining Figure 2 and Tables 8 and 10, PC1 shows negative and small factor loadings for bank NPLs in Malaysia (–0.75) and the Philippines (–0.65), and for MSME exports in Malaysia (–0.76) and Thailand (–0.62); given that PC1 has the opposite sign from the overall estimates, Malaysia and the Philippines contributed to increased bank NPLs by MSMEs in Southeast Asia after the GFC until 2014, and decreased MSME export values in Malaysia and Thailand likely impeded region's MSME development over the period. PC2 suggests that a capital market recovery, especially Thailand's mai and Singapore's Catalist, contributed to the MSME recovery in the region from 2013 to 2015. PC1 also suggests that, after 2016, MSME development in Southeast Asia was supported by an increased number of MSMEs in Indonesia (0.93) and Viet Nam (0.8); nonbank loans in Viet Nam (0.78), Cambodia (0.77), and the Philippines (0.73); and GDP of MSMEs in Indonesia (0.85) and Thailand (0.56).

Table 10: Factor Loadings Based on Probabilistic PCA—Southeast Asia

Country	Variables	PC1
Indonesia	Number of MSMEs	0.93
Indonesia	GDP of MSMEs	0.85
Viet Nam	Number of MSMEs	0.80
Singapore	Nonperforming loans by MSMEs	0.78
Viet Nam	Nonbank loans	0.78
Cambodia	Nonbank loans	0.77
Philippines	Nonbank loans	0.73
Myanmar	Number of MSMEs	0.71
Indonesia	Bank loans for MSMEs	0.69
Viet Nam	Market capitalization	0.68
Cambodia	Nonperforming nonbank loans	0.64
Thailand	Nonperforming loans by MSMEs	0.62
Indonesia	Nonperforming loans by MSMEs	0.59
Thailand	GDP of MSMEs	0.56
Thailand	Number of MSMEs	0.55
Lao PDR	Nonbank loans	0.52
Brunei Darussalam	GDP of MSMEs	0.33
Indonesia	Number of employees in MSMEs	0.30
Philippines	Bank loans for MSMEs	0.26
Myanmar	Nonperforming nonbank loans	0.25
Myanmar	Nonbank loans	0.24
Thailand	Number of employees in MSMEs	0.23
Singapore	Bank loans for MSMEs	0.21
Indonesia	Market capitalization	0.20
Indonesia	Export from MSMEs	0.13
Thailand	Bank loans for MSMEs	0.10
Thailand	Market capitalization	0.05
Viet Nam	Number of employees in MSMEs	0.02
Singapore	Market capitalization	0.00
Philippines	Number of employees in MSMEs	0.00
Lao PDR	Market capitalization	-0.03
Malaysia	Bank loans for MSMEs	-0.08
Singapore	Nonbank loans	-0.12
Malaysia	GDP of MSMEs	-0.13
Philippines	Market capitalization	-0.24
Viet Nam	Nonperforming nonbank loans	-0.25
Philippines	Number of MSMEs	-0.25
Malaysia	Market capitalization	-0.29
Cambodia	Market capitalization	-0.32
Thailand	Export from MSMEs	-0.62
Philippines	Nonperforming loans by MSMEs	-0.65
Brunei Darussalam	Nonperforming nonbank loans	-0.67
Malaysia	Nonperforming loans by MSMEs	-0.75
Malaysia	Export from MSMEs	-0.76
Malaysia	Nonbank loans	-0.77
Brunei Darussalam	Nonbank loans	-0.92

Country	Variables	PC2
Lao PDR	Market capitalization	0.93
Malaysia	Bank loans for MSMEs	0.92
Thailand	Market capitalization	0.83
Indonesia	Number of employees in MSMEs	0.72
Viet Nam	Number of employees in MSMEs	0.60
Philippines	Bank loans for MSMEs	0.58
Singapore	Market capitalization	0.58
Thailand	Bank loans for MSMEs	0.55
Singapore	Bank loans for MSMEs	0.55
Philippines	Number of employees in MSMEs	0.49
Singapore	Nonbank loans	0.48
Philippines	Number of MSMEs	0.43
Viet Nam	Nonbank loans	0.41
Philippines	Market capitalization	0.37
Brunei Darussalam	Nonbank loans	0.35
Indonesia	Number of MSMEs	0.30
Indonesia	Nonperforming loans by MSMEs	0.25
Brunei Darussalam	Nonperforming nonbank loans	0.21
Malaysia	Nonbank loans	0.17
Viet Nam	Number of MSMEs	0.17
Philippines	Nonbank loans	0.15
Brunei Darussalam	GDP of MSMEs	0.08
Thailand	Export from MSMEs	0.04
Thailand	GDP of MSMEs	-0.02
Indonesia	GDP of MSMEs	-0.11
Malaysia	GDP of MSMEs	-0.19
Thailand	Number of employees in MSMEs	-0.26
Indonesia	Market capitalization	-0.27
Malaysia	Export from MSMEs	-0.29
Cambodia	Nonbank loans	-0.32
Malaysia	Market capitalization	-0.34
Singapore	Nonperforming loans by MSMEs	-0.36
Cambodia	Nonperforming nonbank loans	-0.37
Indonesia	Bank loans for MSMEs	-0.37
Myanmar	Number of MSMEs	-0.46
Thailand	Number of MSMEs	-0.47
Cambodia	Market capitalization	-0.52
Philippines	Nonperforming loans by MSMEs	-0.54
Malaysia	Nonperforming loans by MSMEs	-0.58
Thailand	Nonperforming loans by MSMEs	-0.60
Viet Nam	Nonperforming nonbank loans	-0.61
Lao PDR	Nonbank loans	-0.64
Viet Nam	Market capitalization	-0.65
Myanmar	Nonbank loans	-0.69
Indonesia	Export from MSMEs	-0.79
Myanmar	Nonperforming nonbank loans	-0.81

Country	Variables	PC3
Malaysia	Market capitalization	0.74
Cambodia	Market capitalization	0.68
Viet Nam	Nonperforming nonbank loans	0.68
Philippines	Market capitalization	0.61
Myanmar	Nonbank loans	0.59
Brunei Darussalam	Nonperforming nonbank loans	0.58
Singapore	Bank loans for MSMEs	0.55
Singapore	Nonbank loans	0.42
Philippines	Nonperforming loans by MSMEs	0.42
Cambodia	Nonbank loans	0.40
Indonesia	Number of employees in MSMEs	0.40
Myanmar	Nonperforming nonbank loans	0.38
Indonesia	Nonperforming loans by MSMEs	0.36
Indonesia	Bank loans for MSMEs	0.30
Lao PDR	Nonbank loans	0.21
Cambodia	Nonperforming nonbank loans	0.17
Brunei Darussalam	Nonbank loans	0.14
Thailand	Nonperforming loans by MSMEs	0.13
Lao PDR	Market capitalization	0.04
Philippines	Number of MSMEs	-0.01
Thailand	Number of MSMEs	-0.03
Indonesia	Number of MSMEs	-0.03
Indonesia	GDP of MSMEs	-0.05
Thailand	Market capitalization	-0.06
Singapore	Market capitalization	-0.08
Philippines	Number of employees in MSMEs	-0.08
Malaysia	Bank loans for MSMEs	-0.09
Malaysia	Nonperforming loans by MSMEs	-0.09
Viet Nam	Market capitalization	-0.10
Viet Nam	Nonbank loans	-0.11
Malaysia	GDP of MSMEs	-0.12
Malaysia	Nonbank loans	-0.13
Philippines	Nonbank loans	-0.18
Singapore	Nonperforming loans by MSMEs	-0.25
Indonesia	Export from MSMEs	-0.30
Viet Nam	Number of employees in MSMEs	-0.30
Viet Nam	Number of MSMEs	-0.30
Myanmar	Number of MSMEs	-0.31
Philippines	Bank loans for MSMEs	-0.37
Thailand	Bank loans for MSMEs	-0.38
Malaysia	Export from MSMEs	-0.42
Indonesia	Market capitalization	-0.52
Brunei Darussalam	GDP of MSMEs	-0.57
Thailand	Export from MSMEs	-0.67
Thailand	Number of employees in MSMEs	-0.70
Thailand	GDP of MSMEs	-0.71

GDP = gross domestic product, Lao PDR = Lao People's Democratic Republic, MSMEs = micro, small, and medium-sized enterprises, PCA = principal component analysis.
Source: Authors' estimates.

3.   Regional SME-DI: South Asia

In South Asia, nonperforming MSME loans in Pakistan and lower MSME export values in India slowed the region's MSME development after the GFC through 2014. A recovery in capital markets in Pakistan and Sri Lanka, lower nonbank nonperforming loans in Bangladesh and Sri Lanka, increased MSME employment in India, and higher GDP from small manufacturers in Pakistan, all these factors contributed to a recovery among South Asia's MSMEs from 2012 to 2015. After 2016, increased MSME bank loans in India and Bangladesh, nonbank loans in Pakistan and Sri Lanka, and the rising number of MSMEs in Nepal all supported region's MSME development.

Applying the probabilistic PCA to the South Asia subsample, we also obtained the three PC1 to PC3 factors (Figure 3 and Table 11). As summarized in Table 12, the contribution of the three was 88%. PC1 and PC2 for South Asia followed a similar pattern as those in Southeast Asia. PC3 in South Asia had a different pattern from Southeast Asia as well as for the overall estimates. But similar to Southeast Asia, PC3 for South Asia was largely driven by market capitalization, confirming the correspondence between the results in the overall estimates and two subsample analyses.

Examining Figure 3 and Tables 11 and 13, PC1 shows negative and small factor loadings for both bank NPLs by MSMEs and nonbank NPLs in Pakistan (−0.97 and −0.85, respectively), and for MSME exports in India (−0.27); given that PC1 also has the opposite sign from the overall estimates, MSME NPLs in Pakistan and the lower MSME export values in India slowed South Asia's MSME development after the GFC until 2014.

PC2 suggests that a recovery of capital markets in Pakistan (0.82) and Sri Lanka (0.55), fewer nonbank finance NPLs in Bangladesh (−0.71) and Sri Lanka (−0.13), increased MSME employment in India (0.91), and GDP of small manufacturers in Pakistan (0.75) all contributed to a recovery of South Asia's MSMEs from 2012 to 2015.

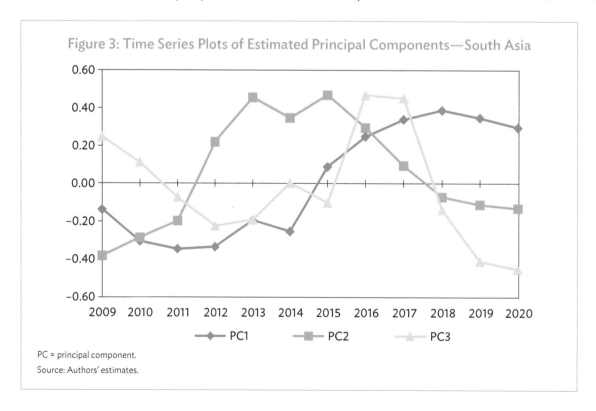

Figure 3: Time Series Plots of Estimated Principal Components—South Asia

PC = principal component.
Source: Authors' estimates.

PC1 also suggests that, after 2016, increased MSME bank loans in India (0.79) and Bangladesh (0.75), nonbank loans in Pakistan (0.87) and Sri Lanka (0.62), and the rising number of MSMEs in Nepal (0.72) all supported region's MSME development.

The regional SME-DI implied that equity finance would be critical for the recovery of MSMEs from the crisis. Once recovered, bank credit and nonbank finance will likely support further MSME development. This suggests finance is critical for MSME development. In particular, delivering growth capital to MSMEs during a crisis would be most effective in helping recovery and growth. This is consistent with key findings from the ASM 2021 Volume 1, which emphasized the need for more growth capital for MSMEs post-pandemic recovery.

Table 11: Time Series of Estimated Principal Components—South Asia

	2009	2010	2011	2012	2013	2014	2015	2016	2017	2018	2019	2020
PC1	-0.14	-0.31	-0.35	-0.34	-0.20	-0.26	0.09	0.25	0.34	0.39	0.35	0.30
PC2	-0.39	-0.29	-0.20	0.22	0.46	0.35	0.47	0.30	0.09	-0.07	-0.11	-0.13
PC3	0.25	0.11	-0.08	-0.23	-0.19	0.00	-0.10	0.47	0.45	-0.14	-0.41	-0.45

PC = principal component.

Source: Authors' estimates.

Table 12: Contribution of Each Estimated Principal Component (3)

	PC1	PC2	PC3
Eigenvalue	4.58	3.10	1.59
Contribution ratio	0.62	0.18	0.08
Cumulative contribution rate	0.62	0.80	0.88

PC = principal component.

Source: Authors' estimates.

Table 13: Factor Loadings Based on Probabilistic PCA—South Asia

Country	Variables	PC1
Pakistan	Nonbank loans	0.87
India	Bank loans for MSMEs	0.79
Bangladesh	Bank loans for MSMEs	0.75
Nepal	Number of MSMEs	0.72
Nepal	Market capitalization	0.63
Sri Lanka	Nonbank loans	0.62
Nepal	Number of employees in MSMEs	0.61
Pakistan	GDP of MSMEs	0.58
India	Number of MSMEs	0.55
Bangladesh	Nonbank loans	0.39
India	Market capitalization	0.32
Sri Lanka	Nonperforming nonbank loans	0.25
India	Number of employees in MSMEs	0.23
Bangladesh	Market capitalization	0.18
Bangladesh	Nonperforming nonbank loans	0.01
Pakistan	Market capitalization	-0.06
Pakistan	Bank loans for MSMEs	-0.16
India	GDP of MSMEs	-0.23
India	Export from MSMEs	-0.27
Sri Lanka	Market capitalization	-0.75
Pakistan	Nonperforming nonbank loans	-0.85
Pakistan	Nonperforming loans by MSMEs	-0.97

Country	Variables	PC2
India	Number of employees in MSMEs	0.91
Pakistan	Market capitalization	0.82
Pakistan	GDP of MSMEs	0.75
Sri Lanka	Nonbank loans	0.73
Sri Lanka	Market capitalization	0.55
Bangladesh	Market capitalization	0.35
Bangladesh	Bank loans for MSMEs	0.21
India	Number of MSMEs	0.18
Nepal	Number of employees in MSMEs	0.13
Pakistan	Nonperforming nonbank loans	0.10
Nepal	Market capitalization	0.02
India	Bank loans for MSMEs	0.01
Pakistan	Nonbank loans	-0.04
Pakistan	Nonperforming loans by MSMEs	-0.05
Nepal	Number of MSMEs	-0.06
Sri Lanka	Nonperforming nonbank loans	-0.13
Pakistan	Bank loans for MSMEs	-0.63
Bangladesh	Nonperforming nonbank loans	-0.71
India	Market capitalization	-0.71
India	Export from MSMEs	-0.74
Bangladesh	Nonbank loans	-0.81
India	GDP of MSMEs	-0.93

Country	Variables	PC3
Pakistan	Bank loans for MSMEs	0.73
Nepal	Market capitalization	0.61
India	Market capitalization	0.56
Pakistan	Market capitalization	0.52
Pakistan	Nonbank loans	0.41
Bangladesh	Nonbank loans	0.17
Pakistan	GDP of MSMEs	0.08
Sri Lanka	Nonbank loans	0.05
India	Number of employees in MSMEs	-0.01
Sri Lanka	Market capitalization	-0.02
Pakistan	Nonperforming loans by MSMEs	-0.02
India	GDP of MSMEs	-0.04
Bangladesh	Market capitalization	-0.07
Pakistan	Nonperforming nonbank loans	-0.09
India	Bank loans for MSMEs	-0.13
Bangladesh	Bank loans for MSMEs	-0.24
Bangladesh	Nonperforming nonbank loans	-0.40
India	Number of MSMEs	-0.55
India	Export from MSMEs	-0.56
Nepal	Number of MSMEs	-0.63
Nepal	Number of employees in MSMEs	-0.67
Sri Lanka	Nonperforming nonbank loans	-0.83

GDP = gross domestic product, Lao PDR = Lao People's Democratic Republic, MSMEs = micro, small, and medium-sized enterprises, PCA = principal component analysis.

Source: Authors' estimates.

4.   Country SME-DI: Viet Nam

In Viet Nam, MSMEs saw higher sales in manufacturing, trade, and transport, and higher employment in trade and agri-food services; profitability in construction improved overall MSME development from 2017 to 2019.

Applying a standard PCA to real data, we estimated the PCs for Viet Nam firm data. There are two main observations.

First, as mentioned, there is no missing industry-level panel data. Thus, we do not need to rely on the probabilistic PCA. This was another test run using a standard PCA to estimate the SME-DI. The same type of test was successfully done in the 2020 SME-DI exercise, but another round of exercise was informative.

Second, applying the probabilistic PCA to the original firm-level data is quite possible. The business registration data accessed contains many missing records for each firm, which theoretically could be handled by the probabilistic PCA. Nonetheless, we did not use it as the size of cross-section (i.e., the number of firms) was much larger than the 3-year time series. In the future we will estimate the SME-DI using the probabilistic PCA and firm-level granular data.

Figure 4 and Table 14 show the PC1 and PC2 factors. First, they show slightly different time-series patterns. PC2 shows a hump-shaped dynamic from 2017 to 2019, while PC1 steadily increases over time. Second, PC1 and PC2 have almost identical contributions to the variation in industry-level panel data, which add up to one (Table 15). Third, there are loadings of each factor for each variable (Table 16). We mark the factor loadings with darker red (blue) color when they have positive and large (small) numbers. The two columns of Table 17 list the loadings that correspond to each factor in descending order. As demonstrated previously, each factor is orthogonal to the other and related to each variable with specific factor loadings. These help analyze each factor.

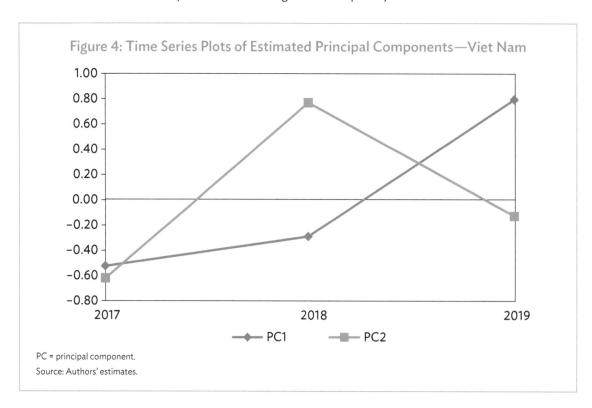

Figure 4: Time Series Plots of Estimated Principal Components—Viet Nam

PC = principal component.
Source: Authors' estimates.

Table 14: Time Series of Estimated Principal Components—Viet Nam

	2017	2018	2019
PC1	-0.53	-0.29	0.80
PC2	-0.62	0.77	-0.13

PC = principal component.
Source: Authors' estimates.

Table 15: Contribution of Each Estimated Principal Component (4)

	PC1	PC2
Eigenvalue	32.28	30.72
Contribution ratio	0.56	0.44
Cumulative contribution rate	0.56	1.00

PC = principal component.
Source: Authors' estimates.

Table 16: Factor Loadings Based on Standard PCA—Viet Nam

Industry	Variables	PC1	PC2
Manufacturing	Total employees	0.45	0.55
	Revenue	0.98	0.02
	Profit	0.04	0.96
Wholesale and retail trade	Total employees	0.99	0.01
	Revenue	0.98	0.02
	Profit	0.07	0.93
Agri-food services	Total employees	0.96	0.04
	Revenue	0.64	0.36
	Profit	0.42	0.58
Construction	Total employees	0.63	0.37
	Revenue	0.00	1.00
	Profit	0.99	0.01
Transportation	Total employees	0.47	0.53
	Revenue	0.92	0.08
	Profit	0.15	0.85
Other services	Total employees	0.42	0.58
	Revenue	0.65	0.35
	Profit	0.03	0.97
Others	Total employees	0.58	0.42
	Revenue	0.79	0.21
	Profit	0.60	0.40

PC = principal component, PCA = principal component analysis.
Source: Authors' estimates.

For PC1, we find the two measures for firm activities, that is, total employees and revenue in the industries, except for construction, are largely associated with the factor. This pattern contrasts with the result associated with PC2 in which profit is mainly explained by the factor, but some is attributed to the number of employees.

Together, these results describe MSME business activity over the 3 years from 2017. Starting in 2017, MSMEs in various industries continuously had higher sales and employment (PC1). The profitability of those MSMEs improved briefly (PC2), but was followed by a slight slowdown potentially due to higher competition, among other issues. Notably, MSMEs in construction showed slightly different patterns of activities such as a revenue peak in the middle of the sample period.

More concretely, PC1 indicated that MSMEs in Viet Nam saw higher sales in manufacturing (0.98), wholesale and retail trade (0.98), and transport (0.92), and higher employment in trade (0.99) and agri-food services (0.96), while profitability in construction (0.99) boosted overall MSME development from 2017 to 2019. Backed by infrastructure development needs and strategies, the national procurement law (Law No.43/2013/QH13 on bidding) offers preferential treatment on domestic bidding to small firms, helping construction-based MSMEs participate in small infrastructure projects; and it likely contributed to overall MSME development in the country.

Table 17: Descending Order: Factor Loadings Based on Standard PCA—Viet Nam

Industry	Variables	PC1	Industry	Variables	PC2
Wholesale and retail trade	Total employees	0.99	Construction	Revenue	1.00
Construction	Profit	0.99	Other services	Profit	0.97
Manufacturing	Revenue	0.98	Manufacturing	Profit	0.96
Wholesale and retail trade	Revenue	0.98	Wholesale and retail trade	Profit	0.93
Agri-food services	Total employees	0.96	Transportation	Profit	0.85
Transportation	Revenue	0.92	Agri-food services	Profit	0.58
Others	Revenue	0.79	Other services	Total employees	0.58
Other services	Revenue	0.65	Manufacturing	Total employees	0.55
Agri-food services	Revenue	0.64	Transportation	Total employees	0.53
Construction	Total employees	0.63	Others	Total employees	0.42
Others	Profit	0.60	Others	Profit	0.40
Others	Total employees	0.58	Construction	Total employees	0.37
Transportation	Total employees	0.47	Agri-food services	Revenue	0.36
Manufacturing	Total employees	0.45	Other services	Revenue	0.35
Other services	Total employees	0.42	Others	Revenue	0.21
Agri-food services	Profit	0.42	Transportation	Revenue	0.08
Transportation	Profit	0.15	Agri-food services	Total employees	0.04
Wholesale and retail trade	Profit	0.07	Wholesale and retail trade	Revenue	0.02
Manufacturing	Profit	0.04	Manufacturing	Revenue	0.02
Other services	Profit	0.03	Construction	Profit	0.01
Construction	Revenue	0.00	Wholesale and retail trade	Total employees	0.01

PC = principal component, PCA = principal component analysis.
Source: Authors' estimates.

Conclusion

This report applied a variant of the PCA method by using two sets of data—the ASM 2021 database and the 2017–2019 Viet Nam enterprise registration data—to estimate an SME-DI regionally and at the country level. Using the method that accommodates missing records in data series, we obtained two or three factors that commonly explain various variables for MSME activities.

For the regional SME-DI, we found that from 2009 to 2020, the region was hit by the GFC with an increase in NPLs, followed by a recovery in capital markets and in corporate financing. For the Viet Nam SME-DI, we found MSME business activities over the 3 years from 2017 to 2019 had higher sales and employment, while profitability improved briefly, followed by a slight reduction.

While this report certainly contributes to the further development of an SME-DI, there are some important remaining issues. First, more data, especially granular firm-level data, are needed for the proposed framework to estimate the factors that represent MSME activities. In the process of managing this project, we tried to access more granular and high-frequency data such as firm-level monthly credit records. Although it was not possible to add much due to resource constraints, a promising way forward is to apply the probabilistic PCA to other datasets to validate its usefulness.

Second, we need to carry out more test runs for additional countries at various levels (aggregate and firm-level). Once we are confident in measuring MSME activities with a small set of indexes and factors, it becomes easier to quickly understand the past and current status of MSMEs. These indexes can help when designing future policies to support MSME development.

Third, after confirming the validity of the SME-DI, future research could have its ability to forecast developments such as the GDP of MSMEs. Regardless of whether using it as an outcome or predictor, a concisely summarized SME-DI is a useful analytical tool to help governments design evidence-based MSME policies.

Appendixes

1. Summary of the Expectation–Maximization Algorithm

A. Expectation–Maximization Algorithm for Complete Data

Algorithm 1 EM Algorithm for complete data

Require: $X, W_0, \sigma_0^2, \text{max\_iter}$

1: **return** $W_{\text{max\_iter}}, \sigma_{\text{max\_iter}}^2$

2: **for** $k = 1, 2, \cdots, \text{max\_iter}$ **do**

3:

4:    ###E Step###

5:    $M_{k-1} \leftarrow (W_{k-1}^\top W_{k-1} + \sigma_{k-1}^2 I)^{-1}$

6:    $<z_i> \leftarrow M_{k-1} W_{k-1}^\top x_i, \quad <z_i z_i^\top> \leftarrow \sigma_{k-1}^2 M_{k-1} + <z_i><z_i>^\top \quad (i = 1, \ldots, n)$

7:

8:    ###M Step###

9:    $W_k \leftarrow \left(\sum_{i=1}^n x_i <z_i>^\top\right) \cdot \left(\sum_{i=1}^n <z_i z_i^\top>\right)^{-1}$

10:   $\sigma_k^2 \leftarrow \frac{1}{n} \sum_{i=1}^n \left(\|x_i\|_2^2 - 2 x_i^\top W_k <z_i> + \text{tr}(W_k^\top W_k <z_i z_i^\top>)\right)$

11:

12: **end for**

B. Expectation–Maximization Algorithm for Incomplete Data

Algorithm 2 EM Algorithm for incomplete data

Require: $X, \mu_0, W_0, \sigma_0^2, \text{max\_iter}$

1: **return** $W_{\text{max\_iter}}, \sigma_{\text{max\_iter}}^2$

2: **for** $k = 1, 2, \cdots, \text{max\_iter}$ **do**

3:

4:    ###E Step###

5:    $M_{k-1} \leftarrow (W_{k-1}^\top W_{k-1} + \sigma_{k-1}^2 I)^{-1}$

6:    $N_{k-1,i} \leftarrow \left(I - (I_i^t)^\top W_{k-1}(W_{k-1}^\top W_{k-1} + \sigma_{k-1}^2 I)^{-1} W_{k-1}^\top I_i^t\right)^{-1} \quad (i = 1, \ldots, n)$

7:    $m_{k-1,i} \leftarrow \begin{bmatrix} W_{k-1}^\top \\ -(I_i^t)^\top \end{bmatrix} (I_i^s s_i - \mu_{k-1}) \quad (i = 1, \ldots, n)$

8:    $D_{k-1,i} \leftarrow \begin{bmatrix} M_{k-1} + M_{k-1} W_{k-1}^\top I_i^t N_{k-1,i}(I_i^t)^\top W_{k-1} M_{k-1} & M_{k-1} W_{k-1}^\top I_i^t N_{k-1,i} \\ N_{k-1,i}(I_i^t)^\top W_{k-1} M_{k-1} & N_{k-1,i} \end{bmatrix}^{-1} \quad (i = 1, \ldots, n)$

9:    $\begin{bmatrix} <z_i> \\ <t_i> \end{bmatrix} \leftarrow D_{k-1,i} m_{k-1,i}$

10:   $\begin{bmatrix} <z_i z_i^\top> & <z_i t_i^\top> \\ <t_i z_i^\top> & <t_i t_i^\top> \end{bmatrix} \leftarrow \sigma_{k-1}^2 D_{k-1,i} + \begin{bmatrix} <z_i> \\ <t_i> \end{bmatrix}\begin{bmatrix} <z_i> \\ <t_i> \end{bmatrix}^\top$

11:

12:   ###M Step###

13:    $W_k \leftarrow \left(\left(\left(\frac{1}{n} \sum_{i=1}^{n} I_i^s s_i <z_i>^\top + I_i^t t_i <t_i z_i^\top> \right) - \left(\frac{1}{n} \sum_{i=1}^{n} I_i^s s_i + I_i^t <t_i> \right) \left(\frac{1}{n} \sum_{i=1}^{n} <z_i>^\top \right) \right)\right.$

14:    $\left. \cdot \left(\left(\frac{1}{n} \sum_{i=1}^{n} <z_i z_i^\top> \right) - \left(\frac{1}{n} \sum_{i=1}^{n} <z_i>^\top \right) \left(\frac{1}{n} \sum_{i=1}^{n} <z_i>^\top \right)^\top \right)^{-1} \right)$

15:    $\mu_k \leftarrow \frac{1}{n} \sum_{i=1}^{n} \left(I_i^s s_i + I_i^t <t_i> \right) - W_k <z_i> \right)$

16:    $\sigma_k^2 \leftarrow \frac{1}{n} \sum_{i=1}^{n} \left(\mathrm{tr}(W_{k+1}^\top W_{k+1} <z_i z_i^\top>) - 2\mathrm{tr}((I_i^t))^\top W_{k+1} <z_i t_i^\top>) + \mathrm{tr}(<t_i t_i^\top>) \right.$

17:    $\left. + \|I_i^s s_i - \mu_k\|_2^2 - 2(I_i^s s_i - \mu_k)^\top (W_k <z_i> - I_i^t <t_i>) \right)$

18:

19:    **end for**

2.   Robustness of the Probabilistic PCA Results in the Regional SME-DI

This appendix provides the results of applying another variant of the probabilistic principal component analysis (PCA) to country-level aggregate data. As opposed to the probabilistic PCA introduced in the regional Small and Medium-Sized Enterprise Development Index (SME-DI) estimates, this alternative method repeatedly applies the singular value decomposition to the data that initially includes missing data and fulfills them. As seen in Figure A.1 and Tables A.1 to A.3, the results obtained are largely similar to those in the overall estimates.

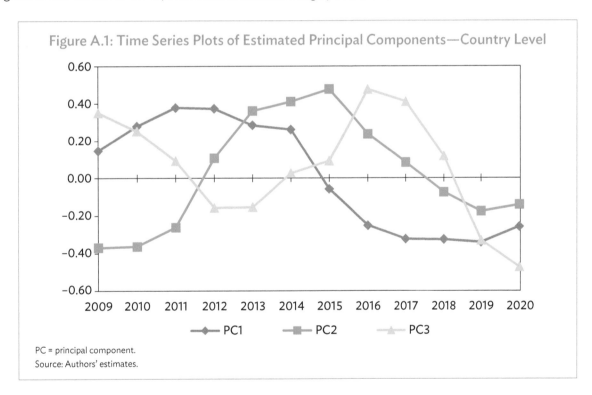

Figure A.1: Time Series Plots of Estimated Principal Components—Country Level

PC = principal component.
Source: Authors' estimates.

Table A.1: Time Series of Estimated Principal Components—Country Level

	2009	2010	2011	2012	2013	2014	2015	2016	2017	2018	2019	2020
PC1	0.15	0.28	0.38	0.37	0.28	0.26	-0.06	-0.25	-0.33	-0.33	-0.34	-0.26
PC2	-0.37	-0.37	-0.26	0.11	0.36	0.41	0.48	0.24	0.08	-0.08	-0.18	-0.14
PC3	0.35	0.25	0.09	-0.16	-0.15	0.03	0.09	0.48	0.41	0.12	-0.33	-0.48

PC = principal component.
Source: Authors' estimates.

Table A.2: Contribution of Each Estimated Principal Component (5)

	PC1	PC2	PC3
Eigenvalue	3.92	2.78	1.73
Contribution ratio	0.33	0.23	0.15
Cumulative contribution rate	0.33	0.56	0.70

PC = principal component.

Source: Authors' estimates.

Table A.3: Factor Loadings Based on Alternative Probabilistic PCA—Country Level

Country	Variables	PC1	PC2	PC3	Country	Variables	PC1	PC2	PC3
Bangladesh	Bank loans for MSMEs	-1.66	0.65	-0.24	Nepal	Number of MSMEs	-1.77	-0.13	-0.84
	Nonbank loans	-1.37	-1.70	0.94		Number of employees in MSMEs	-1.37	0.05	-0.53
	Nonperforming nonbank loans	-0.56	-1.36	-0.76		Market capitalization	-1.82	0.22	1.94
	Market capitalization	-0.46	0.46	0.85	Pakistan	GDP of MSMEs	-1.30	1.55	0.81
Brunei Darussalam	GDP of MSMEs	-0.68	-0.18	0.76		Bank loans for MSMEs	0.51	-3.12	4.16
	Nonbank loans	5.03	3.54	-1.56		Nonperforming loans by MSMEs	6.94	-1.56	1.11
	Nonperforming nonbank loans	1.96	1.54	-2.04		Nonbank loans	-2.16	-0.05	1.69
Cambodia	Nonbank loans	-1.37	-0.66	-0.74		Nonperforming nonbank loans	4.63	0.60	0.06
	Nonperforming nonbank loans	-1.18	-1.03	0.02		Market capitalization	0.06	2.95	2.42
	Market capitalization	1.14	-1.42	-1.53	Philippines	Number of MSMEs	0.37	1.44	-1.56
India	Number of MSMEs	-1.06	0.53	0.48		Number of employees in MSMEs	-0.21	1.30	-1.13
	Number of employees in MSMEs	-0.19	2.48	1.61		Bank loans for MSMEs	-0.46	1.31	-0.43
	GDP of MSMEs	1.16	-4.64	1.16		Nonperforming loans by MSMEs	2.78	-1.45	-3.11
	Export from MSMEs	0.62	-2.18	-1.49		Nonbank loans	-1.81	0.09	1.01
	Bank loans for MSMEs	-1.89	-0.15	0.67		Market capitalization	0.71	1.02	-0.27
	Market capitalization	-1.11	-1.88	2.12	Singapore	Bank loans for MSMEs	-0.75	1.31	-1.43
Indonesia	Number of MSMEs	-1.90	0.41	-0.12		Nonperforming loans by MSMEs	-1.63	-1.43	0.62
	Number of employees in MSMEs	-1.25	2.44	-0.55		Nonbank loans	-0.25	1.87	-2.17
	GDP of MSMEs	-1.60	-0.31	-0.75		Market capitalization	-0.19	1.82	0.14
	Export from MSMEs	0.27	-3.54	0.66	Sri Lanka	Nonbank loans	-1.37	1.39	0.82
	Bank loans for MSMEs	-1.29	-1.28	-0.34		Nonperforming nonbank loans	-0.54	-0.42	-1.27
	Nonperforming loans by MSMEs	-1.49	-0.15	0.52		Market capitalization	3.75	2.15	0.80
	Market capitalization	-0.14	-0.37	-0.21	Thailand	Number of MSMEs	-1.55	-1.98	0.91
Lao PDR	Nonbank loans	-1.04	-1.37	-1.04		Number of employees in MSMEs	-0.48	-0.53	0.23
	Market capitalization	-0.17	4.09	0.79		GDP of MSMEs	-1.05	0.05	0.29
Malaysia	GDP of MSMEs	0.29	0.04	-1.51		Export from MSMEs	3.63	0.54	2.76
	Export from MSMEs	4.16	-0.80	0.09		Bank loans for MSMEs	-0.21	1.54	-0.41
	Bank loans for MSMEs	0.03	2.53	-0.09		Nonperforming loans by MSMEs	-1.47	-1.99	0.16
	Nonperforming loans by MSMEs	6.08	-3.19	-0.22		Market capitalization	-0.24	2.72	1.45
	Nonbank loans	4.20	0.69	2.26	Viet Nam	Number of MSMEs	-1.43	0.21	-0.09
	Market capitalization	0.65	-0.67	-1.65		Number of employees in MSMEs	0.02	2.08	0.72
Myanmar	Number of MSMEs	-1.64	-1.50	0.45		Nonbank loans	-1.76	0.60	0.39
	Nonbank loans	-1.27	-0.97	-2.74		Nonperforming nonbank loans	0.65	-1.26	-2.41
	Nonperforming nonbank loans	-1.20	-1.36	-2.41		Market capitalization	-1.30	-1.58	-0.22

GDP = gross domestic product, Lao PDR = Lao People's Democratic Republic, MSMEs = micro, small, and medium-sized enterprises, PCA = principal component analysis.

Source: Authors' estimates.

References

Asian Development Bank. 2020. *Asia Small and Medium-Sized Enterprise Monitor 2020 Volume IV—Technical Note: Designing a Small and Medium-Sized Enterprise Development Index*. ADB: Manila.

———. 2021a. *Asia Small and Medium-Sized Enterprise Monitor 2021 Volume I—Country and Regional Reviews.*

———. 2021b. ADB Asia Small and Medium-Sized Enterprise Monitor database. https://data.adb.org/dataset/asia-small-and-medium-sized-enterprise-monitor-2021-volume-1-country-and-regional-reviews.

Bishop, C. M. 2006. *Pattern Recognition and Machine Learning*. Springer.

Hastie, T., R. Tibshirani, and J. Friedman. 2009. *The Elements of Statistical Learning: Data Mining, Inference, and Prediction*. Springer.

Tipping, M. E. and C. M. Bishop. 1999. "Probabilistic Principal Component Analysis." *Journal of the Royal Statistical Society. Series B (Statistical Methodology)*. Vol.61 (3). pp.611-622.